PERSPECTIVES
ON HUMAN CONDUCT

PHILOSOPHY
OF
HISTORY AND CULTURE

VOLUME ONE

PERSPECTIVES
ON HUMAN CONDUCT

EDITED BY

LARS HERTZBERG AND JUHANI PIETARINEN

E.J. BRILL
LEIDEN · NEW YORK · KØBENHAVN · KÖLN
1988

Library of Congress Cataloging-in-Publication Data

Perspectives on human conduct / edited by
  Lars Hertzberg and Juhani Pietarinen.

   p.   cm.—(Philosophy of history and culture; v. 1)
  Symposium organized in honor of G. H. von Wright.
  Includes indexes.
  ISBN 9004089373
  1. Man—Congresses. 2. Mind and body—
Congresses. 3. Ethics—Congresses. 4. Wright, G. H.
von (Georg Henrik), 1916- —Congresses. I. Wright,
G. H. von (Georg Henrik), 1916- .
II. Hertzberg, Lars. III. Pietarinen, Juhani. IV.
Series.
BD450.P46225 1988
128'.4—dc19   88-24233
                                             CIP

ISSN 0922-6001
ISBN 90 04 08937 3

PRINTED IN THE NETHERLANDS BY E. J. BRILL

CONTENTS

ACKNOWLEDGEMENTS

The publication of this volume has received financial support from the Åbo Academy Foundation as well as from the Academy of Finland. The editors wish to thank these institutions. We also wish to thank Dr Anthony Johnson for revising the English, Mr Göran Torrkulla for preparing the index, and Mrs Ann-Mari Dahlström and Miss Anitta Lehtonen for typesetting the manuscript. We furthermore wish to express our indebtedness to Dr Lilli Alanen, who took the initiative for organizing the symposium at which these papers were originally presented, and to the Academy of Finland, the Åbo Academy Foundation and the University of Turku Foundation which provided the funds that made the symposium possible.

A different version of 'Moral Conflict and Political Legitimacy' by Thomas Nagel has previously appeared in *Philosophy and Public Affairs* 16 (1987), published by Princeton University Press. 'Who is my Neighbour?' by Peter Winch appeared in his collection of essays *Trying to Make Sense*, published by Basil Blackwell in 1987. The editors wish to thank the publishers for permission to include these essays in the present volume.

INTRODUCTION

Philosophical activity is hampered by borders: by those between various fields of philosophy as well as those between various philosophical traditions. One of Georg Henrik von Wright's virtues as a philosopher is that, in his interests and sympathies, he has consistently flouted them. It therefore seemed a fitting tribute on the occasion of his 70th birthday to organize a symposium in which perspectives on man and human conduct representing various philosophical fields and outlooks would be presented and confronted with one another. The papers presented at the symposium, held at Åbo Academy 26–28 May, 1986, have been brought together in this volume.

It testifies to G. H. von Wright's capacity for intellectual friendship that in organizing the symposium, the speakers to be invited could be chosen from among his personal friends. Indeed, the problem in compiling the list of speakers, if anything, was that of limiting their number. We were happy that von Wright himself agreed to read a paper. The other speakers represented the Federal Republic of Germany, Great Britain, Norway and the United States, as well as Finland.

*

The contributions range from the philosophy of mind and action, over metaphysics to ethics and social philosophy. The volume opens with an interchange between Norman Malcolm and G. H. von Wright, arising out of the latter's Tanner Lectures from 1984, which have appeared under the title 'Of Human Freedom'.[1] The discussion revolves around the mind-body problem, and a central point at issue concerns the nature of human action. Do the reasons and motives expressed in a person's actions have a physiological counterpart? Malcolm argues

---

[1] *The Tanner Lectures on Human Values,* Vol. VI, ed. by S. M. McMurrin (Salt Lake City: University of Utah Press, 1985), pp. 107–170.

that the idea of such a counterpart does not make sense, whereas von Wright is concerned with defending the idea. Frederick Stoutland's contribution, and Lilli Alanen's reply to it, also concern the philosophy of action and the relation between descriptions of action and physiological description. Stoutland argues that the received dichotomy of behaviourism and mentalism is not exhaustive, and he proposes a third possibility which he calls intentionalism. Alanen is substantially in agreement with Stoutland, although she suggests that the question that intentionalism addresses may not be the same as that addressed by behaviourism and mentalism.

Anthony Kenny raises the question of whether the distinction between the Aristotelian and the Galilean traditions of inquiry, as defined by von Wright in his *Explanation and Understanding*,[2] can be applied to the enterprise of trying to make the origins of life and the existence of the universe intelligible. Where the origins of life are concerned, Kenny inclines to the view that they can be made intelligible by an explanation involving causal processes. The origin of the universe, on the other hand, either cannot be made intelligible at all, or else has to be understood "in terms of the purpose of some entity which is not itself part of the material universe".

Jakob Meløe discusses the conditions for being able to observe human actions and the circumstances in which they are performed. He attempts to show how our ability to perceive what someone is doing is in certain cases dependent on our having acquired the ability to participate in the activities in question. The problem addressed by Peter Winch, though it is one that arises in moral philosophy, is at bottom connected with matters discussed by Meløe: Winch makes the suggestion that a person's being prepared to react to a fellow human being in certain appropriate ways (say, to offer him assistance in an emergency) can in a sense be regarded as a condition for saying that he perceives the other as a human being.

Thomas Nagel is concerned with the difficulties involved in the attempt to formulate an impartial standpoint in political conflicts, in particular in the form in which this problem arises for political liberalism. Does the liberal's advocacy, say, of religious toleration commit him to defending the freedom to propagate intolerant religious views? According to Nagel, what we need to realize in order to

---

[2] London: Routledge & Kegan Paul, 1971.

get clear about these issues is that, while liberalism is a substantive moral position, it does not simply compete with specific valuations "as one conception of the good among others": rather, it involves a commitment to the importance of impartiality in assigning weight to diverging valuations.

Albrecht Wellmer, too, raises questions connected with the concept of impartiality in rational argument. How are we to understand Kant's maxim that in order to be rational we must strive to think "from the standpoint of everybody else"? Wellmer brings this question into connection with Wittgenstein's discussions about the conceivability of a solitary language-user. According to Wellmer, the agreement among speakers that is presupposed if there is to be rational argument does not require the possibility of formulating ultimate criteria of truth or rationality. He criticizes the consensus theory of truth in the form developed by Apel and Habermas, on the grounds that it does not yield a test that could actually be applied. Wellmer suggests that, in order to establish that we are thinking from the standpoint of everyone else, we must find out "what the *real* others have to say", and that we must strive to think in ways that are acceptable to all living persons. David Cockburn, in his reply, argues that this suggestion has far-reaching consequences: if I am to regard every respect in which I differ from some other human being as a biasing influence, the matters concerning which there can be rational discussion will be severely limited.

*

There is a type of dichotomy which tends to recur, in slightly varying form, in much traditional and current thought concerning the various forms of human knowledge and its objects, as well as concerning the mind-body problem. We might call it the dichotomy of the physical world as against the human (the mental, intentional or cultural) world. One theme that seems to run through several of the contributions in this volume is the questioning of some of the assumptions convention- ally associated with this dichotomy.

We find a case of this in Malcolm's criticism of the idea that when we use a concept such as understanding in order to explain someone's ability to act in an appropriate manner, the explanation invokes an entity that is "incorporeal" or "immaterial", and hence stands in need of a physiological intermediary if it is to manifest itself in action. What misleads us here, Malcolm argues, is the idea that a condition such as understanding is an entity separate from the particular actions in which the understanding manifests itself. The point could be expressed by saying that, when we use a word like "understand" (or "intend", "believe", etc.), we are not talking about any entity other than the (living) human body. We should keep in mind, nevertheless, that this way of talking about the body has a different logical character from the terminology of muscles and neurons or that of DNA molecules. The idea that talk about corporeal things must always have one logical character, and that that is to be conceived along narrowly physicalist lines, could be said to be the target of Stoutland's discussion. It is this idea which seems to force us to accept the Hobson's choice between behaviourism and mentalism. One expression of this idea, which Stoutland questions, is the notion that "we do not, for example, *observe* in any direct way that people say things, or try to do things, or that someone has a reason for behaving in a certain way. We know these things at most by inference from what we do observe — bodily motions or physical stimuli." It belongs, of course, to the received idea of the physical that only this can be a direct object of observation.

Closely connected with this is the idea that physical objects and events (and only they) present themselves to us in a manner which is independent of our particular perspective on things: while objects and events may be classified and interpreted in a variety of ways, there is a basic level of observation on which their nature will reveal itself in one and the same way to anyone in possession of the requisite sensory capacities (perhaps aided by suitable instruments of observation and measurement). This notion could be said to be implicitly criticized by Meløe. He argues that we are not in a position even to describe "physical objects" such as pieces of furniture or kitchen utensils unless we are familiar with the activities in which they have a use. Thus, only in relation to sitting in a chair does a chair have as much as a particular orientation in space (only by reference to that context can it be said to be standing up, or to have fallen over, or to be turned upside down). This holds for features of our natural environment as well: Meløe gives the example of a rock-climber who is able to see routes, fingerholds and footholds on the rock-face.

There might be an attempt to restrict the scope which has been suggested here for Meløe's argument by claiming that, beside those ways of describing objects which reflect their connection with our activities, there is a form of description which is independent of any particular perspective, the intelligibility of which is made accessible to us simply in virtue of our powers of perception. Meløe does not address this question; it might not be very difficult, however, to formulate an argument designed to show that there could be no teaching and learning of physical descriptions in the absence of a propensity on the part of the learner to act in a variety of ways in accordance with the varying physical conditions obtaining in various situations: to respond recognizably to loud noises and strong smells, to react differentially to heat and to cold, to the softness or the hardness of a surface, etc. If this is so, our physical descriptions may not be intelligible to beings whose patterns of responding (whether from birth or through their having grown up in different environments) are radically different from ours, even if there were no very marked difference in the constitution of their sense-organs. This point is closely related to that suggested by Cockburn in the remark: "If I am to regard all of my reactions to my experience which pertain to myself as an empirical, embodied, being — my spontaneous response to another's smile, my refusal to put my hand in the flame, and so on — as exerting 'a prejudicial influence' on my judgment no room will be left for any thought at all." We may perhaps add that there is one form of this thought about the physical that needs in particular to be resisted: the idea that the natural sciences provide us with a privileged, perspectiveless account of the world. This idea is bound up with the belief that the instruments of observation and measurement employed by scientists put us into contact with things as they are "in themselves", rather than constituting forms of interaction that have been developed for specific practical and not-so-practical ends.

The Editors.

MIND AND ACTION

NORMAN MALCOLM

I

Professor von Wright's Tanner Lectures, entitled 'Of Human Freedom'[1], provide the topic for my essay. Von Wright's main concern in those lectures is the problem of determinism, which I shall not go into. But von Wright also gives an account of human action, which I find extremely interesting and which will be my topic here. Von Wright wishes to clarify the relationship between what he calls "the mental and the bodily aspects" of human action. The relationship that von Wright wants to clarify seems to be similar to something that Hume found "mysterious and unintelligible":

> Is there any principle in all nature more mysterious than the union of soul with body; by which a supposed spiritual substance acquires such an influence over a material one, that the most refined thought is able to actuate the grossest matter?[2]

Hume continues:

> We learn from anatomy, that the immediate object of power in voluntary motion, is not the member itself which is moved, but certain muscles, and nerves, and animal spirits, and, perhaps, something still more minute and more unknown, through which the motion is successively propagated, ere it reach the member itself whose motion is the immediate object of volition. Can there be a more certain proof, that the power, by which this whole operation is performed, so far from being directly and fully known by an inward sentiment or consciousness, is, to the last degree, mysterious and unintelligible?[3]

---

[1] Georg Henrik von Wright, 'Of Human Freedom.' In: *The Tanner Lectures On Human Values,* Vol. VI, ed. by S. M. McMurrin (Salt Lake City: University of Utah Press, 1985), pp. 107–170.

[2] David Hume, *An Enquiry Concerning Human Understanding,* ed. by L. A. Selby-Bigge, 2nd edition (Oxford: Oxford University Press, 1902), Sec. VII, Part I, p. 65.

[3] Hume, op. cit., p. 66.

When a person does a physical act, this requires bodily movement. Normally the person will have reasons and/or motives for his act. Von Wright calls the combination of reasons and motives "the motivational background of an action".[4] He says, rightly, that reasons and motives are commonly called "causes of action".[5] But von Wright, like Hume, is puzzled by the relationship between the "mental" causes of an action (the person's reasons and motives) and the neurophysiological causation of the bodily movements involved in the action. Those movements, says von Wright, are caused by the tension and relaxation of muscles, which are in turn caused by processes in the nervous system.[6]

Thus there appear to be two forms of causation at work in physical action. There is the causation by reasons and motives, and the causation by neural processes. Von Wright insists that there are "conceptual differences between causes of events in nature and reasons for action".[7] Nevertheless, the fact that there are two forms of causation here gives rise to what von Wright calls "a problem of *congruence* or *parallelism*".[8]

> Granting that reasons are causes, we seem to have two parallel but independent causal chains here. On the one hand we have reasons causing actions, and on the other hand we have innervations and other neural processes causing muscular activity. The two chains converge in the physical aspect of the actions.[9]

What does von Wright mean here by "the physical aspect" of an action? Apparently, he means the bodily movements involved in the action. In saying that the two causal chains "converge" in the physical aspect of an action, he would seem to mean that those bodily movements have a "double causation". They are caused by the person's reasons and motives for his action; and they are caused by a chain of causation that starts in the nervous system. Von Wright's idea seems to be that *one and the same thing* is produced by two causal

---

[4] von Wright, op. cit., p. 132.
[5] Ibid., p. 152.
[6] Ibid., p. 148.
[7] Ibid., p. 152.
[8] Ibid., pp. 152–153.
[9] Ibid., p. 153.

chains which exemplify different forms of causation.[10] He presents
"the problem of parallelism" in a striking way:

> When I set myself to act for some reasons, the motivation background
> present in the context of the action "activates me" — and the physical
> aspect of this activation is the "innervations" which make my muscles
> contract and relax and thus direct the bodily movements which consti-
> tute the physical aspect of my action. But how can the motivation back-
> ground which moves *me*, the agent, to action have this power over the
> innervations which move my *muscles* if there is not something answering
> to this background on the physical side, i.e., in the brain or nervous
> system of the agent? The answer, presumably, is that the motivation
> background could *not* have this power unless it had some such "physical
> counterpart".[11]

Unfortunately, something confusing now appears in von Wright's account of "the problem of parallelism". Previously he had said that
we seem to have two parallel but *independent* causal chains, one the
chain of reasons, the other the chain of neural processes.[12] But in
the passage just quoted, he says that the reasons and motives have
"power" over the innervations that move the muscles. If one line of
causation has "power" over another line of causation, then the two are
not *causally* independent. When von Wright said that the two lines
of causation are "independent", did he perhaps mean that they are
"logically" independent but not "causally" independent?

It should be noted that von Wright speaks of only one of these two
lines of causation as having "power" over the other. The reasons and
motives ("the motivational background") have "power" or "influence"
over the neural processes; but there is no suggestion that the latter
have "power" over the former.

Finally, let us note the conclusion that von Wright draws, namely,
that "presumably" the motivational background could not have its
"power" over the innervations that move the muscles, unless there is
a "physical counterpart" of it in the brain or nervous system.

How are we to understand this notion of a "physical counterpart"?
To say that when a person acts from reasons and motives, there is
a "counterpart" of those reasons and motives in his nervous system,

---

[10] Ibid., p. 158. Here von Wright uses the expression "the same reality". In a
letter to me he used the expression "one and the same thing".

[11] Ibid., p. 155.

[12] Ibid., p. 153.

would seem to imply that something *more* is required than that just some neural process or other should cause the bodily movements of the physical action. It seems to be implied that there is a "match" or "fit" between the reasons and motives, and the neural processes. The implication would seem to be that for *every difference* in the reasons and motives for a physical action, there would be *a corresponding difference* in the neural processes that cause the bodily movements of the action. Is this a tenable position?

II

I will consider this question in terms of the following imaginary example. The Master of a certain Oxbridge College traditionally leads the procession of College dons from the Senior Common Room into the Dining Hall at dinner time. When the Master is absent the procession is led by the Senior Tutor. It happens that the Master is frequently absent, whereas the Senior Tutor is rarely absent. A majority of the Governing Board of the College come to feel that it is "not seemly" that which person will lead the procession should depend on the presence or absence of the Master. So the Governing Board passes a ruling that the Senior Tutor shall normally lead the procession, and that the Master, when present, shall place himself at the tail of the procession.

The Master is outraged by the new ruling. After much reflection he decides to refuse to accept it. On the first occasion of his presence in the Common Room after the new ruling, he takes sherry with the dons before dinner, chatting with them in his usual way. When he sees the procession beginning to form, and the Senior Tutor going to the head of the line, he feels a surge of anger. He walks to the head of the line and places himself in front of the Senior Tutor.

There can be different descriptions of what the Master did. He walked to the head of the line; he took his customary place; he defended the Master's ancient privilege; he defied the Governing Board; he expressed his indignation at the new ruling. All of these are true descriptions of what the Master did. The last three descriptions are more explicit about what was momentous in the Master's action. The Master had walked to the head of the line hundreds of times previously; but never before had his doing this produced consternation among the dons.

It could be that the Master's bodily movements were just the same as they had been many times previously. His walking was not especially rapid nor especially slow. The steps he took were neither longer nor shorter than usual. There might have been nothing unusual in his facial expression, nor in the rapidity of his breathing.

Yet the assembled dons would perceive his walking to the head of the line as an *action of defiance*. They would perceive it that way because they know the *special circumstances*. They are familiar with the ancient tradition; they are aware of the new ruling of the Governing Board; they anticipate the Master's indignation. Of course they did not *know* that the Master would *defy* the Governing Board; but now they see it happening.

In contrast, a visitor who knew nothing of those special circumstances, would not, indeed *could not*, perceive the Master's walking to the head of the line *as an act of defiance*. This would be so, even if the visitor had, by virtue of some advanced technical apparatus, a vast knowledge of what was going on in the Master's nervous system! I won't here say anything in defence of this last assertion.

I want to use the example of the Master's act of defiance to test von Wright's suggestion that when a person acts from reasons and motives, there is a "physical counterpart" of those reasons and motives in the person's brain or nervous system. The meaning of this idea is very obscure. What can be the sense of speaking of a neural "counterpart" of reasons and motives? But, as I said previously, this does seem to *imply* that if the reasons and motives were different then the neural counterpart would be different, i.e. there would be some difference in the neural processes.

This seems highly unplausible when we think of the example of the Master. His bodily movements on that occasion *might* have been no different from what they were hundreds of times previously when he walked to the head of the line. If we are to assume, as von Wright does, that the Master's bodily movements were caused by neural processes, then if the bodily movements were the same as before, why should the neural processes be different? Of course they *might* be different; but is there any ground for *presuming* that they would be different?

When the Master had walked to the head of the line on previous occasions, what were his reasons and/or motives for doing this? The question is puzzling. What can we say, other than that it was the tradition in the College that when the Master was present he would lead the procession? He was just acting in accordance with his role as the Master. But on the momentous occasion, his reasons and motives for walking to the head of the line were entirely different. He was indignant at the new ruling of the Governing Board; he wanted to defend the ancient privilege of the Master; his intention was to defy the Governing Board by taking his customary place at the head of the line.

On this occasion his walking to the head of the line was an act of defiance. Never before had it been so. The action was different even if the bodily movements were the same. There is no justification, on *conceptual* grounds, for thinking that the difference in action required a difference in the *neural causation* of the same bodily movements.

In order to try to get a grip on von Wright's idea that "presumably" to the reasons and motives for an action, there corresponds a neural "counterpart", I drew from it the implication that when the action is different the neural processes will be different. If that is a correct implication, then the idea is untenable. I doubt that any *philosophical* argument can establish that there is a correlation between the reasons and motives for action, and the neurophysiological processes that cause bodily movements.

I am trying to show that there is no philosophical basis for believing that there is the problem which von Wright calls "a problem of *congruence* or *parallelism*".[13] This is presented by him as a problem of understanding how two different lines of causation (one of reasons and motives, one of neural processes) "converge in the physical aspect" of an action.[14]

Von Wright appears to believe that there is some "one and the same thing" that is causally explained by two different causal explanations. *What* is this "one and the same thing"? Von Wright says that it is "the physical aspect" of an action. What does he mean by "the physical aspect" of an action? In one place he says that "the bodily movements... constitute the physical aspect" of an action.[15] In other places he says that "the muscular activity" is the physical aspect of

---

[13] Ibid., pp. 152–153.
[14] Ibid., p. 153.
[15] Ibid., p. 155.

an action.[16] Perhaps by "the muscular activity" he just means "the bodily movements". I will not try to decide this. I will assume that by "the physical aspect" of an action, he means either muscular activity, or bodily movements, or both.

How does von Wright arrive at the idea that the aforesaid two different lines of causal explanation converge in "the physical aspect" of an action? Do not the reasons and motives explain *the action*? And do not the neural processes explain *something different*, namely, the muscular activity and/or the bodily movements? Von Wright's answer, surprisingly, is that these are the same thing! He says that "the muscular activity" and "the action" are "the same reality".[17] He says: "The action is not anything over and above its physical aspect ...".[18]

On the other hand, von Wright also says that an action is *not identical* with its physical aspect.[19] For this he gives the very good reason that no description of the muscular activity or bodily movements would suffice to *identify* the action.[20]

So von Wright is saying *both* that an action and its physical aspect are "the same reality", *and* that the action and its physical aspect are *not identical*. It is his inclination to think that an action and its physical aspect are "the same reality" that leads him to think that two lines of causation *converge* in one and the same thing. That same thing may be called either "the action" or "its physical aspect", since these terms refer to "the same reality". What are we to make of this? How can it be that the action and its physical aspect are *not identical*, and yet are "the same reality"?

III

I am grateful to Professor von Wright for bringing these conflicting inclinations to the surface. At one time I struggled with these same opposed inclinations. The problem, as I stated it, was whether there could be both a "purposive explanation" and a "neurophysiological explanation" of one and the same behaviour. In the essay I published

---

[16] Ibid., e.g., p. 157.
[17] Ibid., p. 158.
[18] Ibid.
[19] Ibid.
[20] Ibid.

I concluded that there *could* be.[21] Subsequently I came to think that this was a mistake. Let us consider this issue in relation to the example of the Master.

One description of what the Master did is that he defied the Governing Board. The explanation of his action, under that description, is to be found, not in the neural causation of his bodily movements, but in the previous circumstances, i.e. the existence of the ancient tradition, the new ruling of the Governing Board, the Master's indignation, and his decision to defy the ruling.

Another description of what the Master did is that he expressed his indignation at the new ruling. Once again, his action under this description cannot be understood in terms of the neural causation of bodily movements, but only in terms of those previous circumstances.

A third description of what the Master did is simply that he walked to the head of the line. In the context of the situation, this description says something about the goal or intention of the Master's walk, namely, to place himself at the head of the line. The neural causation of his bodily movements cannot account for his intention *to place himself at the head of the line.*

So far we have found no place for neural processes in the explanation of what the Master did.

But of course there could be a description of the details of the Master's bodily movements as he walked to the head of the line. It might be that he took steps of 30 inches in length. Perhaps there might be a neurophysiological explanation of why his steps were of precisely that length. But the motivational background we have assumed would offer no explanation of the length of his steps. There could be a case in which the Master intentionally took 30 inch steps; but that is not our present case.

I am unable to discover any point at which there is an "overlapping" or "convergence" of two different lines of causal explanation, one an explanation in terms of reasons and motives, the other an explanation in terms of neural processes.

Consider von Wright's own example of unlocking a cupboard in order to take out a bottle of wine for dinner. Suppose that his wife had previously said to him, "You know that guests are coming for dinner.

---

[21] Norman Malcolm, 'The Conceivability of Mechanism', *The Philosophical Review* 77 (1968).

Have you opened a bottle of wine?"; and that he had replied, "Oh, no.
I must do that", and then had gone to the wine cupboard. Given those
circumstances it would be easy to identify the action he was engaged in
at the cupboard door. But merely from an observation of his muscular
activity and/or bodily movements, or from a knowledge of his neural
processes, one could not identify his action — as von Wright himself
declares.[22]

Then why does von Wright say that the action, and its "physical
aspect", are "the same reality"? This is his explanation:

> The action is not anything over and above its physical aspect, if by "over
> and above" one understands some thing or some event in the physical
> world which one could identify as that which, when "added" to the
> muscular activity "makes up" the (whole) action.[23]

Now of course what constitutes the action is not the addition of
some physical event, nor indeed of some mental event, to the bodily
movements. But it seems to me to be confusing and misleading to
conclude from this that the action and the bodily movements are "the
same reality", or "one and the same thing".

I think that what is not receiving sufficient attention in von Wright's
account of action is the part that *the circumstances, the situation,
the context,* play in making something the action that it is. Has not
von Wright taken account of this in speaking of "the motivational
background"? No: for he means by this only the reasons and motives
that "made the agent act or moved him to action".[24] Von Wright also
employs the phrase "the *context* of an action". But what he means
by this, it seems, is just what is involved in the physical process of
the action, including the innervations of the muscles, and the bodily
movements, ending in the completion of the action.[25]

What I mean by "the context" is different. It is the notion of "the
circumstances", "the situation", "the surroundings", "the context",
that comes from Wittgenstein, and on which he puts great emphasis.
He says:

---

[22] von Wright, op. cit., p. 158.
[23] Ibid.
[24] Ibid., p. 132.
[25] Ibid., pp. 153-154.

> An intention is embedded in its situation, in human customs and institutions. If the technique of playing chess did not exist, I could not intend to play a game of chess.[26]

Wittgenstein's work abounds with illustrations of how something that goes on in a space of time would have an entirely different significance if placed in different surroundings. A man sits in his room hoping that a friend will bring him some money: but in different surroundings, where there was no institution of money, that hope could not exist. At a coronation the crown is being placed on the head of the king in his coronation robes: a scene of pomp and dignity. But in different surroundings, where gold is the cheapest of metals and its gleam is thought vulgar; where the fabric of the rope is cheap to produce, and a crown is a parody of a respectable hat — this would be a scene of derision and ridicule.[27]

The same consideration obviously applies to the concept of action. In the example of the Master an important feature of the context or situation is the existence of the ancient tradition that the Master leads the procession of dons, and another is the ruling of the Governing Board. Neither of these are things that occurred during the Master's walk to the head of the line: but if they had not been part of the surroundings, then the Master's action would not have been a defence of the tradition, nor an act of defiance. Neither the tradition nor the ruling belong to the "context" of the action in von Wright's sense of this word. Nor are they part of what von Wright calls "the motivational background" of the action. They were not, in themselves, either reasons or motives. They are what *gave rise* to the Master's motives and reasons for what he did.

It seems to me that once we have a clear perception of the crucial role that the *surroundings* (including previous events, and long-standing traditions, institutions, practices) play in *defining* what a person did on a certain occasion, then we shall no longer be inclined to think that an action and its physical aspect (bodily movements and/or muscular activity) are "the same reality" or "one and the same thing". When that inclination is undermined then there is no case left for thinking that there is "a problem of congruence or parallelism". There

---

[26] Ludwig Wittgenstein, *Philosophical Investigations*, trans. by G.E.M. Anscombe (Oxford: Basil Blackwell, 1953), Part I, para. 337.
[27] Ibid., para. 584.

is no sound basis for thinking that there is some one and the same thing (the physical aspect of an action) on which both "purposive" causation and neural causation "converge".

IV

Although I believe there is no genuine "problem of parallelism", as conceived of by von Wright, it is of interest to consider how he proposes to deal with this supposed problem. He speaks of "the parallelism between the reasons (motivation background) of an action and the innervations and neural patterns causally responsible for its physical aspect".[28] He wants to *explain* why it is "no 'accident' that when the reasons move the agent, the causes of muscular activity move his body 'correspondingly'".[29] What is his explanation?

It goes like this: As a person grows up in a community he learns a lot of language and a lot of ways of responding to language. During this period of learning and development the person's nervous system is being prepared or "programmed". Von Wright says that, for example,

> In order to understand commands... I have to learn a language and to react to orders and other messages... and this process involves a (physical) impact on my nervous system. My brain becomes programmed to certain reactions to stimuli.[30]

Thus there are supposedly *two* processes that occur simultaneously as a person grows and learns: a development of his knowledge and understanding, and a development of his nervous system. Von Wright says:

> When an infant grows up to be a member of a society, learns to speak and to do various things, to understand the meaning of challenges and institutions, and to participate in various practices, its nervous apparatus undergoes a simultaneous development partly of learning under the influence of external stimuli and partly of maturation of inborn capacities. The two processes go hand in hand and therefore the congruence between the mental and the bodily aspects of action is a *harmony* established in the course of the individual's life and necessary for its preservation over the span of time allotted to each of us.[31]

---

[28] von Wright, op. cit., p. 157.
[29] Ibid., p. 161.
[30] Ibid., p. 156.
[31] Ibid., p. 162.

Von Wright divides the parallelism or harmony between the "mental" and the "bodily aspects" of action into three parts. He says:

> To the *understanding* of the reasons (as reasons for or against an action) there answers a programming of the neural apparatus, and to the *existence* of the reasons in the context of a certain action there answers a stimulation of this apparatus, and to the agent's proceeding to action there answer innervations of some muscles in the agent's body.[32]

In these remarks von Wright is using the word "answers" to mean *corresponds*.

Previously I argued that there are no conceptual grounds for supposing that there is a "correspondence" between the reasons for an action and the neural processes that are presumed to cause the bodily movements involved in the action. The argument was that different actions, done for different reasons, can involve the same bodily movements, and that those same bodily movements *could*, presumably, have the same neural causation. Now in the passage just quoted von Wright is assuming *another* correspondence: a correspondence between a person's *understanding* the reasons for an action and a "programming" of his neural apparatus.

I do not see that the notion of such a correspondence is even intelligible. This notion *seems* to assume that when a person understands the reason for an action, his understanding that reason is some definite process or state that is present in him as long as he understands the reason. Why do I say this? For the following reason: if the nervous system receives such-and-such a programming, it is put into a certain definite state that will remain until there is a breakdown or else until that "programme" is removed. If there is a "correspondence" between a "programme" and the understanding of something, then it would seem that the understanding and the "programme" would have *simultaneous duration*. As long as the programmed state of the nervous system is continuously present, so will the understanding be continuously present.

Let us consider an example. The pupils in a school are instructed as to how they are to respond when the alarm bell rings. They are told that they are to file out of their classroom in an orderly way and to proceed out of the building. The teachers require the pupils to repeat the wording of that instruction. In addition there are drills in which

---

[32] Ibid., p. 157.

the exercise of vacating the building is practised. The teachers are eventually satisfied that their pupils understand what their response to an alarm bell should be.

Do we have to assume that this understanding is some process or state that is continuously present, consciously or unconsciously, in the minds of the pupils, throughout the school year? Surely not.

The pupils understand that the sound of the alarm is a reason for leaving the building. On what do the teachers base their judgment that the pupils have this understanding? First, on the fact that the pupils give a correct answer to the question, "What are you supposed to do when the alarm sounds?". Second, and more importantly, on the fact that the pupils *act* in the appropriate way when drills occur.

Why does a pupil walk out of the building in a quiet and orderly way when the alarm sounds? Because, due to the instruction and training, he understands that he should act that way. Isn't that an adequate explanation? A pupil who had not received that training would probably either remain in the classroom or else rush about the building in a panic.

But there is a philosophical inclination to feel that the training and consequent understanding, *by themselves,* are *not* an adequate explanation of the pupil's behavioural response. One may feel that a required effect of the training is to produce a "programming" of the pupil's neural apparatus. This programming is an *intermediary* between the training and the appropriate behaviour. When the programmed neural apparatus is stimulated by the sound of the alarm, this results in neural impulses that bring about the bodily movements which are involved in walking out of the building in an orderly way. If it were not for the *intermediary* (the programming), the training of the pupils would not have the desired effect.

Von Wright says that the "programming of the nervous system" is not a *conceptual* requirement: it "is a matter of *empirical* (scientific) and *not* conceptual knowledge".[33] But the belief in a neural programming *corresponding* to one's understanding of something is *not* based on scientific knowledge. No neurophysiologist has discovered a correlation between a person's understanding some particular thing and a specific state of the person's neural system. The idea that there *needs to be* such a correlation is philosophical, not empirical.

---

[33] Ibid., p. 156.

This idea is similar to the belief in *physiological memory-traces.* Many psychologists and philosophers *take it for granted* that if I had a certain experience a month ago, I could not recall it today — unless it was "deposited" in my nervous system in some form or other and "retained" there throughout the month. This view is not taken because physiological memory-traces have been *discovered.* No. Memory-traces are postulated *a priori* as a *requirement* for remembering. The feeling is that remembering *without* memory-traces would be "magical" and therefore unintelligible.

I hazard the guess that something similar underlies von Wright's thinking on the present topic. Suppose that I start out to do some physical action for reasons and motives. Von Wright wonders why it was that *just then* there occurred those neural impulses which caused the bodily movements that were the "physical aspect" of my action? His answer is that "presumably" there was in my nervous system a "physical counterpart" of my reasons and motives.[34] Why does he say "presumably"? There is no *empirical* basis for this presumption. It has an *a priori* look.

V

I suggest that in our philosophical thinking about "mind and action" we have a strong tendency to picture the matter in the following way: When a pupil comes to understand the meaning of the alarm bell, his understanding of that is something essentially "mental" — and *as such* it will not produce the appropriate physical action when an occasion for it arises. It will not *move his limbs*! Only if his understanding is supplemented by a physical counterpart of it in the nervous system will the pupil *act* as he should.

But it is a mistake to think of the pupil's understanding as essentially "mental" — in *that* sense. Understanding is conceptually connected with *doing.* A pupil could not be said to "understand" the meaning of the alarm if he did not ever say or do the right thing. The conceptual link between understanding the meaning of the alarm and the appropriate behaviour is too strong to leave any place for the question, "Why did the pupil act as he did?". There can be no justified demand for an "intermediary" that is "correlated" with the

---

[34] Ibid., p. 155.

pupil's understanding of what he is supposed to do. In the example of the Master we know *why* he walked to the head of the line. We do not need to "fill in" the account by postulating a neural state or process that is a "counterpart" of the Master's motives for his action.

In *Zettel* Wittgenstein makes a penetrating observation about the philosophical belief in psycho-physical parallelism. He says:

> The prejudice in favour of psychophysical parallelism is a fruit of primitive interpretations of our concepts. For if one allows a causality between psychological phenomena which is not mediated physiologically, one thinks one is professing belief in a gaseous mental entity.[35]

By the "prejudice" or "bias" (*Vorurteil*) in favour of parallelism, Wittgenstein means the non-empirical *assumption* that for each psychological phenomenon there must be a correlated neural phenomenon. What does he mean by "a causality between psychological phenomena"? Well, that is one of the ways in which we use the word "cause". For example, we can say of the Master that his *decision* to defy the Board was *caused* (was *brought about*) by his *indignation* at the new ruling. This is an illustration of causality between psychological phenomena.

The belief in parallelism is inspired by the feeling that such causality must be "mediated physiologically". Why should we think so? Here is where a "primitive interpretation" of our concepts plays a role. When we think of our psychological concepts as referring to phenomena that are "incorporeal" or "immaterial", it seems to us that they are too "vaporous" or "gaseous" (*nebelhaft*) to *cause* anything! In order to make it intelligible to speak of "causality" here, we assume something like the following: A neural process "corresponding" to the Master's indignation, caused a neural process "corresponding" to his decision, and perhaps this latter neural process caused "the physical aspect" of his action of defiance. We feel that his indignation and his decision, in themselves, could not have brought about something so physical as the Master's walk to the head of the line.

This philosophical picture of psychological phenomena is remote from our everyday knowledge. We all know that rage can cause acts of physical violence, that the fear of heights can prevent one from walking on the edge of a cliff, that pity can produce acts of kindness.

---

[35] Wittgenstein, *Zettel,* trans. by G.E.M. Anscombe (Oxford: Basil Blackwell, 1967), para. 611.

In everyday life we constantly explain physical behaviour in terms of psychological causation. We do not think of rage, fear, or pity, as too "nebulous" to cause physical action.

I do not think that the notion of a "physical counterpart" in the nervous system, of reasons and motives, is intelligible. But without going further into that, what I am arguing is that the postulation of these neural counterparts is uncalled for, not needed. The conceptual connections between psychological phenomena and human physical actions are *sufficient* to account for the causation of those actions. I mean, for the *whole* of those actions, not just for their "mental aspect".

*

I wish to end with a comment that pertains to the purpose of this colloquium, which is to honour Georg Henrik von Wright. Georg Henrik and I have enjoyed a personal and philosophical friendship for forty years. On the philosophical side of that friendship we have often agreed and sometimes disagreed. In either case I have greatly profited from our exchanges of ideas. In regard to this difficult topic of "mind and action" it is possible, or even probable, that I have not understood Georg Henrik. Whether or not this is so, I have no doubt that at the bottom of our apparent disagreement there is some deep confusion that entangles both of us.

REFLECTIONS ON
PSYCHO-PHYSICAL PARALLELISM

G. H. VON WRIGHT

I have been hesitant whether I should confine myself to a reply to Malcolm's paper or give an independent talk on the same, or a closely related, topic. In the end I opted for the second alternative. But first a few words about my reaction to Malcolm.

I

With much of what Malcolm said I agree — also with certain things on which he seems to think that we do *not* agree, perhaps because unclear expressions or infelicitous metaphors made my thoughts liable to misunderstanding. I shall not, however, attempt to correct them here.

Some of Malcolm's critical points are well taken and will force me to withdraw some of my statements in the Tanner Lectures as being either misleading or, quite frankly, false. His most important criticisms concern my attempts to describe the conceptual situation in which the problem of psycho-physical parallelism, as I see it, has its roots. About the solution to that problem or perhaps better: about how to cope with it, there seems to exist genuine disagreement between Malcolm's approach and mine.

To Malcolm the idea of "parallelism", i.e. of a neural counterpart to all so-called psychological phenomena, seems not to make sense, to be unintelligible. Once it has been shown that and why it is nonsense, the idea "dissolves". To me too the idea is confused. But my attitude is that it contains an important grain of possible truth. Therefore, instead of debunking it as nonsense, I should like to state it in a way which makes its meaning clear and removes the "mystification" of which it has been the source. I am not sure that I can do this, even to my own satisfaction, within the scope of this paper. But I shall make a modest effort.

However, my lecture has also another aim. As Malcolm noted at the beginning of his talk, *my* main concern in the Tanner Lectures was the problem of freedom and determinism. Malcolm did not go into it. This I shall do, however. My reason is that the problem of determinism is intimately connected with that facet of the problem of psycho-physical parallelism for which Fred Stoutland has coined the name "problem of congruence". I shall begin with an attempt to describe wherein *this* problem consists and how I propose to solve it.

II

Every human action has what elsewhere I have called a *somatic* (bodily, physical) aspect. That this is the case I shall regard as a conceptual (intrinsic, logical) truth about action.

The somatic aspect of an action consists in muscular activity — usually in some movements of parts of the body, but sometimes also in the restraining of movements. Of this activity the agent is often aware and he can, "in principle", control it. If asked why the activity occurred on a given occasion, he can usually explain — for example by giving a motive or reason for an action of which the activity is the somatic aspect. It is not unnatural to call the reason the "cause" of the activity in question.

On the other hand the muscular activity is also thought — and probably rightly so — to be caused by processes in the agent's nervous system. I shall refer to them as "innervations". Of them he is *not* aware — and whether he can be said to "control" them is at least uncertain. The innervations may in their turn have (physiological) causes of their own — and these causes may be traced back to events (stimuli) affecting the nervous system from outside the agent's body. The existence of such chains of ever remoter causes of the somatic aspect of an action may not be a conceptual necessity (although many philosophers seem to believe this). But it surely is an empirical possibility. This being accepted, we face the following situation:

The somatic aspect of an action may have causes which are independent of the actions of the agent and unknown to him. In the light of these causes the somatic aspect of his action seems "predetermined". On the other hand, it occurred because of a reason which the agent had for an action (of which it is the somatic aspect). There is thus a kind of "double causation" involved. The question arises whether this is compatible with our notion that an agent is "free" when he acts.

One cannot answer or dismiss the question by saying that the reason "causes" the *action* and the innervations and their remoter causes cause its *somatic aspect.* True, the action is not the same as, "identical with", its somatic aspect. But this aspect belongs to the action *intrinsically.* If we ask what the action itself *"is"* over and above its somatic aspect, the answer must be something like this: it is *intentional* movements (or restraining of movements), i.e. movements which occur because of an intention, or reason, or want of an agent. So we are inevitably faced with the fact that those same movements occur, on the one hand, because of some reason for producing them and, on the other hand, because of some physical causes operating independently of the agent. Can anybody accept this without a feeling of puzzlement? At least I cannot do so.

There are some traditional shortcuts to a solution which have been tried, but which I find unacceptable myself. One is to tamper with the idea of causality — for example by introducing a notion of "agent-causality" which is supposed to be efficacious in moving the body and, maybe, even "retroactively" to have power over the innervations which "steer" the muscles. Or one tampers with determinism by postulating indeterminism at the level of microevents which occur in the human nervous system. Such "loopholes" in nature's causal chains I cannot accept as aids to a solution of the philosophical puzzles relating to the notion of human freedom. But this does not mean — be it said in passing — that I myself believe in "rigid determinism" in nature. I even doubt whether *this* idea can be given an intelligible expression, — except as an empty truism.

In fact, I think I now see my way out of the difficulty. I shall imagine a concrete situation — less dramatic than Malcolm's brilliant story about the college master and also simpler but not, I think, unduly simplified to be a good example of acting for a reason. I sit in my room, hear a knock on the door, get up and open the door. If asked why I did this I would say in reply something like "there was a knock" or "somebody knocked". The knock gave me a reason for opening the door. This presupposes not only that I *heard* the knock but also that I *understand* the "meaning" of door-knocks. Proceeding to open a door upon hearing a knock is not a "reflex", but an "action". If challenged,

I could also say something about *why* hearing a knock is a reason for opening the door. Presumably someone was anxious to see me, had some message for me or wanted to ask me something. It is part of my upbringing that one lets the person in unless, of course, one has some good reason against doing so. A reason against could be that I am too busy, or that I do not wish to be disturbed, or that I fear something unpleasant and want to give the stranger the impression that I am not in the room. And there may be other reasons as well for not responding.

The story I have told should make us aware of the distinction between *having* a reason for an action and *acting* on a reason — between a reason "existing" and a reason being "operative". This distinction will help us to see what it is to *understand* something as a reason for an action. It is, if not the only one, then at least a very important aspect of what it means to "understand" something as a reason for an action that, *in the absence of reasons against,* one proceeds to the action. Perhaps one does not succeed, but one makes at least an effort. Not "invariably" perhaps, but certainly "normally".

Thus, if I have no strong reason against responding to the knock, I open the door. Imagine the following conversation in a case when I don't respond. "Did you not hear the knock?" "Yes." "Don't you understand what it 'means'?" "Yes." "So why did you not open?" This last question "obliges" me to explain my passivity by giving a reason for *it*. If in many cases when I am challenged I cannot explain why I did not respond one would begin to doubt whether I understand the significance of knocks on doors — and perhaps eventually conclude that I do *not* understand this.

Is not understanding something "mental"? Certainly it is not a "mental state" or "mental process". Nor is it "thinking" or "being aware". It presupposes that I have learnt something and that I am able to "account" for what I understand, if challenged. And, in the case we are discussing, an important "component" of the understanding is action. Thanks to this, my body is also involved, *intrinsically,* in my understanding.

Also in the *presence* of reasons against, it may happen that I act. My action is then usually the outcome of deliberation or the result of a decision. With this aspect of action I shall not be concerned here.

In our example the reason for my action was given to me, came into existence, thanks to my hearing a knock — and it was operative, let us assume, thanks to the fact that I had no reason against responding. I suppose that all reasons for, or against, individual actions which we have, originate in something which happens to us — usually something in the so-called external world, something we see or hear or are being told, but sometimes also "inside" us as when we feel thirsty and go for something to drink. One can refer to that which gives us the reason (brings it into existence) as a *stimulus,* and to the action as a *response.* The relation between these two is "mediated" by our understanding of the stimulus as a *reason* for the response.

It is essential that the stimulus be "received" by the agent. A knock on the door does not "by itself" give me a reason for acting. I must also hear it. I must not be deaf or so absorbed in some other activity that I do not notice it. This is yet another way in which my body is involved in the context of my action.

If I heard a knock, there presumably *was* a knock, i.e. somebody or something hammering on the door, thereby producing a sound perceived by me as a knock. This is not always so, however. I open the door and find nobody there. I would then, giving a reason for my action, say something like "I *thought* I heard a knock" or "it *seemed* to me that somebody was knocking". But before opening I would have said simply "I heard a knock". Nothing in my "mind" has changed, — but I find myself in a new situation the correct description of which necessitates a certain modification in the description of my earlier situation.

One cannot "think that one hears a knock" unless one has not already heard a good many knocks (in the past). And certain auditory sensations would not be perceived as door-knocks unless there were not many other things in the world with which one is familiar not only through hearing but also through seeing them and having learnt to react to them in manifold ways.

Now let us have a look at what happens in the nervous system in the acting-situation which begins with my hearing a knock and terminates in my opening a door. Vibrations in the air produced by something hitting a door were propagated to my ears, affected the hearing nerve, "released" in it electro-chemical processes which were then propagated through the nerve cells to the sensory centres of the brain. Here, in the central region, the processes were, somehow, shifted over, "mediated" or transmitted to the motor centres causing in them outgoing processes, "innervations". Those processes were propagated to the muscles and effected in them contractions and relaxations in a combination answering to the movements I performed in getting up from the chair, advancing to the door, seizing the handle, turning it and pushing, or pulling, the door open. This is a very much contracted and simplified, "unscientific", description of an extremely complex process which normally involves also feedback stimuli from sensations of an optic and haptic character. But never mind the simplifications! The purpose of the description is to remove the appearance of a conflict between freedom and determinism produced by the fact that one and the same event in the world, viz. the somatic aspect of an action, may, on the one hand, have neurophysiological causes and, on the other hand, make its appearance under the impact of reasons for acting. The impression of a conflict vanishes when we consider that existing reasons for a performed action have a causal origin in the very same events in the physical world, say a knock on a door, which are also ultimately responsible for the movements which constitute the somatic aspect of this action.

The events or processes in the physical world which explain how an agent came to have the reasons on which he acted may in their turn have causes operating prior to the agent's coming to have the reasons. Perhaps this is *usually* the case. A believer in determinism would say that it is *always* and necessarily the case. This may be an overstatement, but none the less it is seldom "mere chance" that an agent happens to have the reasons for action which he actually has. This, however, does not mean that he does not, in normal cases, "really" act for (because of) reasons. The causal account which we think we can give of how an agent came to have the reasons on which he acted would sometimes show that the agent was, as we say, a "victim" of circumstances over which he did not have control. We might deny that he was free to do what in fact he did. This would be a perfectly acceptable and common use of the word "(un)free" when applied to agents and their actions. But the agent all the same *acted* (for some reasons) and did not *just* "react" with his body to some stimuli. In this sense he was *free*. If free agency means acting because of reasons, there is no logical incompatibility between freedom and (even) the strictest possible form of (physical) determinism. To think otherwise is simply a confusion.

So much for the problem of "congruence". I now turn to that of "parallelism".

III

Let us once again look at what happens in the agent's nervous system in the action situation which we have been discussing. So far we have heard only the beginning and the end of the story: the processes transmitting the "message" from the ear to the hearing centre and the innervations transmitting the "order" from the centre to the muscles. These are also the scientifically best known parts of the story. But is has also a middle part, linking the beginning with the end: the "decoding" of the message from the senses as an order to the muscles. In mentalistic terms this means understanding the sound as a reason for opening the door. The neurophysiological details corresponding to this part of our story are, for all I know, largely obscure even to science. *I* have no idea what they are. Nevertheless I shall give free rein to my imagination in trying to think what they *may be*.

The motor reaction to the sensory stimulus is not inborn. It has to be acquired through learning. Once learnt, it becomes what I propose to call "quasi-automatic" in the sense that it will normally follow in the absence of reasons against the action. It is not too unlike that which physiologists and psychologists call a conditioned reflex.

It does not seem to me at all unnatural to think that to learning how to react to a knock on the door there corresponds some *restructuring* in the central nervous system. Some connections between nerve fibres which did not previously exist become established and enable the brain to *function* in a new way. I do not say that it *is* so — only that I fail to see why it could not be so.

But what about the cases when there are reasons against the action? The existence of those reasons also has a causal history, analogous to the causal history of the normal reason *for* the action. We come to have the contrary reasons because of something which happens to us and the meaning of which as a signal *not* to open the door we understand in the same way as we understand the knock as a signal to open it. Also to the acquisition of this other understanding correspond structural features of the brain with functional capacities responsible for the "operation" of the contrary reasons. We can imagine that when no action takes place, the connections which mediate between the auditory stimulus (hearing the knock) and the motor reaction (opening the door) are *blocked* because of the way in which these other connections then function. Let me indulge in the following fantasy:

Acquiring understanding of some stimulations as reasons for or against an action corresponds to the installation in the brain of a system of traffic-lights, red and green lamps, which are turned on and off as the reasons are being given (occur) to us. When the reason-giving stimulus occurs and there are no reasons against the action (already "stored in the brain"), the green light permitting the sensory impulses to proceed to the motor grooves is turned on. A red lamp already burning would indicate the presence of a counter-reason blocking the passage. But whether the red light is on or not may depend, not only on the existence, but also on the *strength* of the counter-reason, for example on the degree to which the agent is fatigued or otherwise disinclined to react.

Of course I do not believe that there are such red and green lights in the brain. I *know* there are no such things! But the idea (thought, imagination) that there is *something* analogous to this constellation of structural and functional units in the brain does not seem to me "unintelligible" ("meaningless"). It seems to me even rather plausible. Not only for door-opening in response to knocks, but generally for actions and omissions because of reasons. And I would be willing to generalize it to the entire range of so-called psychological phenomena. Sensations and perceptions, recollections and thoughts, reasons for action may all have distinct physical "counterparts" in the neural system without which those psychological phenomena would not occur with the person who has them.

Again, I do not say that it *is* so — only that it *may be* so. I see no way of refuting the conceptual possibility. Nor do I see any reason for thinking that it is not also a *physical* possibility, i.e. any reason for thinking that its truth would conflict with well established laws and principles of natural science. To entertain the possibility as a truth is to entertain it as a scientific *hypothesis*. In view of its general and vague nature it would be better to call it a scientific *research programme* or *heuristic idea* guiding physiological and psychological investigation. As such it may be interesting and valuable. It is not certain, however, that the research programme can be carried out beyond a certain limit without *conceptual* innovations — of which, moreover, I think there are some signs in contemporary physics and biology. Conceptual change and development in science are also of interest to philosophy since they may have repercussions both on our view of the world and understanding of man's place in it. But no such conceptual innovations are needed in order to save us from being snared in determinism or reduced to "mere" automata or machines. These dangers are the product of conceptual confusion and misunderstanding. But conversely, no future "brain research" will — contrary to what many enthusiasts now seem to expect — eventually solve "the riddle of consciousness". This too is a philosophic muddle which no findings of a scientific nature will ever clarify.

IV

To regard psycho-physical parallelism as a logical and also physical possibility is thus to view it as that which I think it basically *is*, viz. *a scientific* "theory". But this is hardly, or at least not exclusively, how it has been viewed by those who have either acclaimed or disputed its importance as a *philosophical* position. In philosophy, the issue is not so much whether psycho-physical parallelism is a logical and physical possibility as whether it is a conceptual, and in that sense "logical", *necessity.*

My stand on this question is perhaps obvious from what I have already said. But something has still to be added.

Even if one denies that it is a conceptual necessity that all psychological phenomena have a counterpart in the nervous system, it is of interest to ponder what can be the philosophic *motivation* behind this view. I think the motivation has been exposed rather clearly by Norman Malcolm in his paper. It is the idea that we could not *understand* the psychological phenomena — perceptions, thoughts, volitions, etc. — i.e. understand their existence, occurrence, "possibility" — unless we postulated for them a correspondence or foundation in the brain. Like Malcolm I think such postulation unwarranted. But to see this clearly is perhaps not easy; I still have some difficulties here.

I think it is right to say that what happens when a person, say, *hears* something, *understands* something, and *does* something is completely intelligible without any reference to what goes on in his nervous system. From the point of view of understanding this, it is irrelevant whether the person in question *has* a nervous system at all. Suppose that an autopsy revealed that he in fact had no brain inside his skull, or no nerves from his ears to the cortex or from there to the muscles. We should of course be immensely surprised. Surely we should say, quite justifiedly, that we do not *understand* how it was *possible* for him to hear and respond to what he heard with an action. The case requires an explanation. What we want to explain then is how *he* could hear and act in spite of these abnormalities in his anatomy. The question concerns the *physical,* not the logical, possibility of hearing and acting with a person whose bodily constitution is, in the said respect, abnormal. *That* he heard and acted when alive we need not doubt later on. He had ears and limbs. When alive he reacted to sounds just as normal people do. Our astonishment is at the fact that he *could* hear and act. *Perhaps* there is an explanation for this. In lower animals even very important functions of some damaged or missing organ can be taken over by some other organ; why could this not be the case, "in principle", with man and his brain too? (Of course, this *is not* so.)

In order to understand what it *is* to hear we need no physiological theory of hearing. We can teach a child what it is to hear without having to mention nerves, but *not* without mention of ears and macroscopic bodily reactions to sound. And the same for action. That there is hearing and acting, and that we have all the criteria we need for deciding in the individual case whether these phenomena occur is all that is needed to establish their *logical* possibility. *"Ab esse ad posse valet consequentia"* as the Schoolmen put it. What is true of hearing and acting for reasons is also true of other perceptual, intellectual, emotional, volitional, etc. psychological phenomena. Once this is seen and admitted, the *philosophical* motivation behind the psycho-physical parallel theory is, I think, demolished.

V

Just as it is intrinsic to the notion of an action that an action has a somatic aspect, it is intrinsic to the notions of hearing and seeing that a man has ears and eyes ("sense organs"), intrinsic to the notion of perceiving that his body is oriented towards other objects in space,

intrinsic to the notion of learning to grasp meanings that he is exposed
to influences from and interacts with his surroundings. The full story
of the agent who opened a door in response to a knock is an intrinsic
mixture of features, some of which belong to what we call his mental,
others to what we call his bodily life. That the mixture is intrinsic
means that the two aspects cannot be separated and the full story
told exclusively in terms belonging to one or to the other of them.

The fact that the story has intrinsic features some of which relate to
the bodily, others to the mental life of the person is itself a "psycho-
physical parallelism" of a sort. Not, of course, of the sort which usually
goes under that name. But because of this mixture of physical and
psychological features one may also doubt whether the term "psycho-
physical parallelism" is appropriate for the contingent correspondence
(which I have here been considering under that name) between the
story's intrinsic features and the correlated extrinsic data relating to
that which is and happens in the persons's nervous system in an action
situation. The traditional picture of the parallelism surely is different:
on the one hand a robust physical reality of neurophysiological and
-anatomical facts, on the other hand an ethereal, incorporeal reality of
something called mental phenomena. Stock examples of the latter are
things such as "being in pain" or "having an optical after-image". Or
one speaks abstractly about "states of consciousness" as though this
most obscure term had a clear meaning. This idea of psycho-physical
parallelism is often, even if not always and necessarily, coupled with a
thesis to the effect that the parallelism amounts to an *identity* between
the mental phenomena and their neural equivalents.

Of *this* idea, both that of parallelism and that of identity, I would
say that I find it unintelligible, a conceptual confusion, — and *here* I
think I agree with Norman Malcolm.

RESPONSE TO GEORG HENRIK VON WRIGHT

NORMAN MALCOLM

Professor von Wright holds that there is no "conceptual necessity" that when a person acts from reasons and motives there is a "physical counterpart" of those reasons and motives in his nervous system. But he does think there *may be* a such a counterpart. It is a "conceptual possibility". It does not appear to him that this notion is unintelligible. Instead it is "even rather plausible" (p. 29). He is willing to extend the notion of a possible physical counterpart to "the entire range" of "psychological phenomena":

> Sensations and perceptions, recollections and thoughts, reasons for action, may all have distinct physical "counterparts" in the neural system, without which those psychological phenomena would not occur with the person who has them (ibid.).

I would not say that this notion is "plausible", since this word suggests that there is some sort of *evidence* for it. There is no doubt, however, that it is *appealing*. But one thing we learn in philosophy is that an idea may be appealing, yet nonsensical. For example, the idea that each person "knows only from his own case" what the words "anger", "fear", "pain", etc., *mean,* is certainly one of the most attractive, even *compelling,* ideas in rudimentary philosophical thought — which is one reason why Wittgenstein devoted so much energy and ingenuity to displaying its nonsensical character.

The main problem with the notion of psycho-physical parallelism is to *understand* it. How is von Wright using the word "counterpart"? He is implying, in the above quoted remarks, that when for example I perceive something (say, a squirrel's leap from one branch to another) there *may* be a counterpart of that perception in my neural system. How are we to understand the expression "x is a counterpart of y"?

There is a common use of this expression in which it means: x and y have the same function. For example, Mr. A. is an official in the British Embassy whose function is to control the issuing of passports. Mr. B. is an official in the French Embassy whose function is the same.

It could be said to Mr. A.: "Your counterpart in the French Embassy is Mr. B.". This meaning of the word "counterpart" seems, however, to have no application to the relation between my perception of the squirrel's leap and its supposed neural counterpart. What does it mean to speak of "the function" of a perception, recollection, thought, or reason? Does *every* perception have "a function", or only some of them? In the absence of an explanation of that expression for this context, it is impossible to understand the statement that a perception and a neural state or event *may* have "the *same* function". I am not ascribing this meaning of "counterpart" to von Wright — but I am trying to show the haziness of his use of that expression by mentioning an ordinary use of it which is not suitable for his purpose.

There is something in von Wright's wording which suggests that by the neural "counterparts" of psychological phenomena he might mean: those conditions that are *necessary* for the occurrence of the psychological phenomena. For he says that *without* the putative "counterparts" in the neural system "those psychological phenomena would not occur" (ibid.). There were, however, many conditions of different sorts necessary for the occurrence of my perception of the squirrel's leap. For example, that I was awake; that I can distinguish squirrels from birds; that I was looking in that direction; that I had an unobstructed view; that I was not distracted by troubling thoughts — to mention a few. I am sure that von Wright would not want to say that any of those necessary conditions for the occurrence of the perception was a "counterpart" of the perception. Apparently there is something in the notion of a "counterpart" that is not caught by the idea of a necessary condition. Nor would it be of any help to suppose that a "counterpart" would be the *totality* of necessary conditions: for such a totality (if it makes sense at all) would include conditions that are not neural ones.

It could be that the notion of a neural counterpart is linked to the so-called "principle of psycho-physical isomorphism". Wolfgang Köhler was a prominent exponent of this "principle". What it meant for him was that whenever "experiences" occur, they are matched by simultaneous, *structurally identical,* neural states or processes. Köhler used the word "experiences" to cover sensations, perceptions, thoughts, emotions, recollections, and so on. His term "experiences" appears to have the same extension as von Wright's phrase "psychological phenomena".

Could von Wright's suggestion that psychological phenomena *may* have neural "counterparts" amount to a tentative endorsement of "the principle of psycho-physical isomorphism"? Perhaps. If so, von Wright's suggestion would imply that a perception, for example, has a *structure*; and his inclination to think that there may be a "counterpart" of the perception in the nervous system, would be the inclination to think that there may be a neural state or process which is "identical in structure" with the perception.

I have criticized "the principle of psycho-physical isomorphism" in detail elsewhere.[1] I will not repeat that discussion, but will mention one point. The notion that a psychological phenomenon such as a perception or recollection, is or has "a structure", strongly appeals to the imagination of philosophers and psychologists. If you think that *of course* a recollection or perception has a structure, then you are at least half-way to the opinion that a neural state or process might have the *same* structure.

To say that something has a "structure" surely implies that it has *parts* or *elements*. If we ask, "What were the elements of my perception of the squirrel's leap?", we may realize, perhaps with a shock, that we have no idea how to answer this question. We don't know what to count as "the elements" of that perception, or of any other perception, recollection, or thought. When we realize that there is no ready answer, we may feel that the philosophical picture of a psychological phenomenon as a "structure", collapses or fades away, and with it "the possibility" that something in the nervous system may have "the *same* structure".

We could of course *stipulate* that the elements of a particular perception are such & such. But once started on that path we would see that the stipulations could be made in different ways, thus yielding different structures for one and the same thing. So to talk about "the structure" of a psychological phenomenon is either meaningless or uninteresting. It is the first if we don't know what to count as "the elements" of the supposed structure; it is the second if we see that we could specify "the elements", and therefore "the structure" in indefinitely many ways — with the result that anything could have "the same structure" as anything else.

---

[1] See my *Memory and Mind,* (Ithaca & London: Cornell University Press, 1977), especially Chap. 10, 'The Principle of Isomorphism'.

If von Wright's idea that there *may* be a neural "counterpart"
for each psychological phenomenon is an inclination to accept "the
principle of psycho-physical isomorphism", then I don't believe there
is much future in it for either science or philosophy.

I will not continue these speculations about how von Wright's term
"counterpart" is to be taken. I will end by saying, not that the notion
of a neural counterpart of a psychological phenomenon is *intrinsically*
unintelligible (whatever that might mean), but by saying that the
notion is without sense until it is *given* sense — and giving it sense
will not be easy.

ON NOT BEING A BEHAVIOURIST[1]

FREDERICK STOUTLAND

The desire not to be a behaviourist, which of late has been commendably strong, is often accompanied by the belief that in order not to be a behaviourist one must be a mentalist. This belief is not objectionable if being a mentalist simply *means* not being a behaviourist, but if it means something more — as it usually does — then it makes any other way of not being a behaviourist impossible. This is objectionable because it may be that behaviourism and mentalism share common assumptions, assumptions which ought to be rejected, and if that is so, there must be a better way of not being a behaviourist.

This is what I shall argue for by considering, from the perspective of the philosophy of action, not only the mentalist alternative to behaviourism, but another conception of action which I shall call "intentionalism". Both mentalism and intentionalism object to behaviourism for leaving out everything but the physical in its account of human behaviour. Mentalism objects that behaviourism leaves out the mental causes of human behaviour. Intentionalism — a point of view I first learned from Georg Henrik von Wright[2] — objects that behaviourism fails to recognize that human behaviour cannot even be adequately described in purely physical terms, something which mentalism also fails to recognize.

The majority of philosophers today are mentalists, and the position is so well established it usually goes unargued for. One reason is that

---

[1] Some parts of this paper also appear in my 'Three Conceptions of Action', which is forthcoming in *Pragmatik*, Vol. III, ed. H. Stachowiak (Hamburg: Felix Meiner Verlag). That paper is less compressed and less technical and contains many more references; it may, therefore, be useful to persons unfamiliar with recent discussions in the philosophy of action.

[2] See especially his *Explanation and Understanding* (Ithaca: Cornell University Press, 1971) and *Freedom and Determination (Acta Philosophica Fennica* 31, No. 1, 1980). For further references see my 'Davidson, von Wright, and the Debate over Causation' in G. Fløistad, ed., *Contemporary Philosophy: A New Survey*, Vol. 3 (The Hague: Martinus Nijhoff, 1982), pp. 45–72.

mentalism underlies cognitive science, which has become a powerful movement impatient to get on with what it sees as a research programme that, belonging to what Kuhn called "normal science", should not have to examine its philosophical assumptions. To understand the force of mentalism, therefore, we shall have to consider its role in cognitive science.

My underlying aims in this paper are three: 1) to examine some assumptions basic to mentalism and, therefore, to cognitive science, from the point of view of philosophy of action[3]; 2) to discuss some of the difficulties mentalism faces; and 3) to consider why mentalism, in spite of its difficulties, is so widely believed to be the only alternative to behaviourism. I shall argue that mentalism shares with behaviourism a crucial assumption that behaviour and the world in which agents act are merely physical, an assumption which is deeply entrenched, but which should be rejected in order to clear a space for intentionalism as an alternative to both behaviourism and mentalism.

I.   Behaviourism

Let me begin with some remarks on behaviourism. It is distinguished not by its emphasis on observable behaviour but by its claim that behaviour can be adequately described and explained in physical terms alone. By "physical terms" I mean terms which do not involve the meaning or significance phenomena have for agents or in a world of agents. They do not, therefore, involve agents' intentional attitudes, the role or value of phenomena in social, cultural, or historical settings, or the assessment of behaviour as rational or irrational. Terms which do involve these matters I shall call "intentional": they apply to phenomena in terms of the meaning phenomena have for agents as participants in communal structures.

This distinction between the intentional and the merely physical is not sharp, and my characterization is very rough, but I don't know how to do better without begging all sorts of questions. I think it

---

[3] I shall refer to two recent works in cognitive science: Steven Stich's *From Folk Psychology to Cognitive Science* (Cambridge, Mass.: MIT Press, 1983) and Zenon Pylyshyn's *Computation and Cognition* (Cambridge, Mass.: MIT Press, 1984).

is enough for our purposes.[4] It subsumes the familiar distinction between action descriptions and bodily movement descriptions. It subsumes the cognitive science distinction between semantic, content or cognitive terms on the one hand and syntactic, functional, or computational terms on the other.[5] We might characterize it as the distinction between terms which figure essentially in the physical sciences — as they have been conceived since Galileo — and those which do not. The physical sciences do not, for example, characterize behaviour as rational or irrational; that requires reference to a world of agents within which behaviour can be rational or irrational. In this respect physical science since Galileo is rather different from physical science under the influence of Aristotle, where "physical" simply meant "natural" and where explanations in intentional terms

---

[4] The distinction is problematic and it may be that it should be abandoned or radically re-shaped; my excuse for retaining it is that it is relied on by behaviourists and mentalists. This use of "intentional" came into the current discussion via Brentano. There is a useful recent discussion in D. Dennett, *Content and Consciousness* (London: Routledge and Kegan Paul, 1969), Chap. 2. See also Donald Davidson, *Essays on Actions and Events* (Oxford: Clarendon Press, 1980), pp. 210 ff. Davidson generally uses "psychological" or "mental" as synonyms for "intentional". At the Åbo Symposium Peter Winch argued that this use of "physical" is very specialized — that only physicalists speak of a "physical language", for example — and that to adopt it is already to grant too much to the physicalist assumptions of both behaviourists and mentalists. I think this is right, but I decided to go with the current philosophical practice of using "physical" instead of the more accurate "physicalist". Had I adopted Winch's suggestion, my basic thesis might have been put by saying that we should reject the assumption, common to both behaviourists and mentalists, that descriptive terms are either physicalistic or mentalistic — that it is precisely that distinction which creates the illusion that we must be either behaviourists or mentalists.

[5] Cf. Pylyshyn, op. cit., esp. Chap. 2. The contrast between semantic, content, or cognitive terms and syntactic, functional, or computational terms is not the same as that between the intentional and physical because, strictly speaking, the latter are not physical terms. They rather describe phenomena in terms of what John Haugeland calls *medium independence*, which means they describe them independently of how the phenomena are realized and, therefore, independently of whether they are realized physically. I won't worry about this distinction here, however, because these terms are like physical terms in being non-intentional, and no one who uses them thinks they are realized in any other way than physically. For the reference to Haugeland, cf. his *Artificial Intelligence* (Cambridge, Mass.: MIT Press, 1985), p. 58 ff.

of natural phenomena were accepted.[6]

The behaviourist programme was to establish *laws* connecting environmental stimuli with behavioural responses. Many philosophers saw this as a reductive programme, but for psychologists it was not a matter of giving physical definitions of intentional terms but simply a matter of doing without them — on the sensible ground that if laws were to be established, stimuli and responses would have to be described in physical terms. For while there are innumerable correlations between environmental stimuli and behavioural responses — for example, drivers stop at corners where there are stop signs, people park where the police tell them to, animals deprived of food attempt to eat — these are in intentional terms and are not exceptionless or law-like. The hope was that if both behaviour and its environment could be re-described in purely physical terms, law-like correlations could be established.[7]

I won't detail the familiar problems with the programme, which can be summed up by saying that behaviourism was able to establish law-like correlations only in carefully contrived experimental set-ups which ensured that physical (or functional) descriptions of a subject's behaviour were extensionally equivalent to intentional descriptions — which ensured, for example, that there was essentially only one set of bodily movements which could constitute a rat's seeking food. But this meant that intentional descriptions, even of non-humans, still played an essential role in the correlations, so that it could not be ruled out that any success behaviourism had rested on a surreptitious re-introduction of intentional terms. What was being explained, in other words, was not the rat's behaviour described in bodily movement terms — not the motions of the rat's limbs — but behaviour described in intentional terms — the rat's behaviour under the description "seeking food"[8] — and what were functioning as explanatory stimuli were not environmental conditions specifiable in purely physical (or func-

---

[6] For a perspicuous discussion of this point, cf. Chap. I of von Wright's *Explanation and Understanding.*

[7] On the claim that laws require physical terms, cf. Davidson, *Essays on Actions and Events*, esp. pp. 211 ff.

[8] Even though in this case, because of the experimental set-up, what were described as the motions of the rat's limbs and what were described as its seeking food happened to be the same events. Explanation is not of events *per se* but of events as described in certain ways (of events under a description).

tional) terms, but conditions specifiable only in such intentional terms as "something to eat". But it was precisely such intentional terms which behaviourism proposed to do without.[9]

II.   Two responses to behaviourism

Both mentalism and intentionalism accept this criticism of behaviourism, and both see it as flawed in excluding any concept of behaviour as intentional. Both can also accept the claim that behaviour is intentional under a description if and only if the behaviour is performed for reasons — if and only if it has a rational explanation. This requires two things: that there are reasons in the light of which the behaviour is rational, and that those reasons explain the behaviour in terms of the description under which it is intentional.

I shall assume that the idea of behaviour as intentional under a description is acceptable. That behaviour is intentional *if* it has a rational explanation I take to be non-contentious. That it is intentional *only* if it has a rational explanation is more controversial, and I do not think it can be accepted without qualification, but the qualifications do not affect the burden of this paper nor distinguish mentalists from intentionalists.[10]

But mentalists differ from intentionalists in the way they understand what a rational explanation is. Mentalists hold that reasons explain behaviour only if they cause it, the difference between merely having reasons and acting on them being a *causal* difference. Reasons one merely has are rationalizations; only reasons that cause behaviour explain it. And since behaviour is intentional (under a description) if and only if explained by reasons, behaviour is intentional if and only if caused by reasons.[11]

---

[9] For an excellent statement of this criticism of behaviourism, see D. Dennett, *Brainstorms* (Cambridge, Mass.: Bradford Books, 1978), esp. pp. 13–15 and 53 ff.

[10] That intentional action must have a rational explanation has been defended by Davidson on numerous occasions. See *Essays on Actions and Events*, e.g., p. 85. I think the claim is too strong; there are, for example, intentional actions done for no (particular) reason.

[11] The term "cause" is often used simply as a synonym for "because". The issue between mentalists and intentionalists is not over "cause" in this broad sense, for both hold that agents act because of their reasons (and in *that sense* both hold that reasons cause actions). The sense of "cause" here and throughout this paper is a narrower sense in which it presupposes relations which are law-like and rest on

The claim that causation is the *only* way to distinguish explanation from rationalization and therefore the only way to mark out behaviour as intentional under a description is seldom argued for explicitly. Its plausibility comes from background assumptions. They manifest themselves here in the very way the question about the intentionality of behaviour is posed. I take this question to be, "What are the conditions for behaviour being intentional under a description?" Mentalism construes that question in a distinctive way — namely, "What are the conditions for behaviour, *identified and described in purely physical terms* as bodily movements, also to be intentional under a description?" This assumes that behaviour described in terms of bodily movements is what is given to observation, so that it is behaviour identified and individuated as a set of bodily movements about which we are asking whether *it* is intentional under a description. Behaviour, therefore, will be intentional under a description only if we can find conditions under which bodily movements are intentional. The only candidates are either their causes or their effects. But the intentionality of bodily movements cannot consist in their effects; effects could at best be evidence that they were intentional. The only plausible candidates are causes. A causal answer is forced just by the way the question of intentional behaviour is posed.

The background assumption here is that all observational terms are physical, so that observations of behaviour must be expressed in physical terms. This is the basis of the characteristic mentalist way of responding to behaviourism's exclusion of intentional terms. Mentalism criticizes the behaviourist programme for resting on an operationalist philosophy of science which excludes intentional terms because they are non-observational, and it responds by arguing that intentional terms refer to *inner* states which, mediating between observable stimuli and responses, are not themselves observable. Behaviourism's fundamental difficulty, in other words, is its commitment to a discredited operationalism, which leads it to exclude terms whose referents are unobservable inner states.

Many mentalists — certainly those committed to cognitive science — see this point about inner states as the key to realizing in a new way

---

empirical generalizations — the sense of "cause" in which antecedents necessitate their effects.

the behaviourist quest for law-like correlations between environmental stimuli and behavioural responses. The correlations are not direct, but involve inner states as intervening variables. Moreover — and this is what cognitive science takes as original about its programme — the inter-connection of inner states is not law-like in the usual sense but *computational*.[12] There is, nevertheless, a connection between stimuli and responses which satisfies the ideal of physical science that all connections satisfy an algorithm.

Having made this move, it might occur to someone that these inner states themselves are describable in non-intentional terms, so that the behaviourist ideal of excluding intentional terms is disentangled from its operationalism. This idea did occur to Stephen Stich — he calls it the "syntactic theory of the mind"[13] — but it has not been widely accepted by other cognitive scientists, who argue that intentional terms are not eliminable and must have referents, namely, these inner states.[14]

The idea that intentional terms refer to inner states fits in with the causal account of reasons by showing how reasons can be causes, namely, by being inner states. For mentalists, reasons are inner states with content in the light of which behaviour is rational and which cause that behaviour. So conceived, reasons must be inner states of *individual* agents. It cannot, for example, be the policeman telling me to park there that is my reason for parking there, for that is not an inner state; my reason must be my belief that the policeman told me to and my desire to obey him. It cannot be the stop sign on the corner which is the reason for people stopping there; it must be desires and beliefs present in individual drivers. Mentalists *internalize* and *individualize* all reasons.

Now some brief comments on intentionalism. It holds that reasons may explain behaviour even if they do not cause it. The distinction between reasons which are mere rationalizations and those which are explanations need not involve causality — either as evidence for applying the distinction or as its truth conditions. Reasons are linked with the behaviour they explain in a variety of ways, ranging from

---

[12] For a lucid discussion of what this means, see John Haugeland, 'The Nature and Plausibility of Cognitivism' in Haugeland, ed., *Mind Design* (Cambridge, Mass.: MIT Press, 1981).

[13] Stich, op. cit., Chap. 8.

[14] See, for example, Pylyshyn, op. cit., Chaps 1 and 2.

principles of logic through the sort of practical wisdom we may not be able to articulate.

Its fundamental objection to behaviourism is not that it neglects the unobservable causes of behaviour but that it assumes that if intentional terms refer at all they must refer to what is unobservable. Intentionalism argues, on the contrary, that we *observe* directly not only physical motions and events but behaviour as intentional. We observe that persons are greeting each other, taking notes, trying to open windows, not merely that their bodies are moving.

From this point of view, mentalism grants too much to behaviourism, for in holding that intentional terms refer only to inner states, it grants the point that physical terms alone are adequate to describe behaviour and the environment in which agents behave. Intentionalism argues, on the contrary, that intentional terms apply directly to observable behaviour and to its environment, which are, therefore, intentional, and not merely physical phenomena.

III.   Difficulties in mentalism

Mentalism's central thesis in philosophy of action is that behaviour is intentional (under a description) if and only if caused by inner states in the light of whose content the behaviour is rational. The most natural way of construing this is in terms of the "covering law model" of causality because it allows for an intelligible connection between being a cause and being a reason. According to this model, behaviour is intentional if and only if there is a *causal law* connecting the content of the reasons — of the agent's beliefs and desires — with the description under which the behaviour is intentional. Beliefs and desires are both reasons and causes insofar as they cause the agent's behaviour *in virtue of being* reasons for it. Not only can the agent's behaviour be considered rational in the light of her reasons, but the very features of those reasons in the light of which it is rational — i.e., their contents — figure, so it is claimed, in a causal law which also includes a description under which her behaviour is intentional.[15]

---

[15] For this point of view, see, for example, C. G. Hempel, 'Rational Action', in *Readings in the Theory of Action*, ed. by Care and Landesman (Bloomington: Indiana University Press, 1968), pp. 281–305.

The advantage of this account is this intelligible connection between being reasons and being causes, which would explain why behaviour with rational causes is intentional, namely, because the content of the reasons is connected by causal law with the description under which the behaviour is intentional. Reasons which are mere rationalizations, on the other hand, do not constitute behaviour as intentional since their content is not part of a causal law covering the agent's reasons and the descriptions under which her behaviour is intentional.

The disadvantage of this account, however, is that it requires causal laws we do not have. I shall not review the arguments for this because the point is widely accepted and there are now few defenders of the covering law account of how reasons are causes. In philosophy of action most of the arguments involved versions of the "logical connection argument", and while not all versions of that argument were cogent, its central critical point — namely, that there are no causal laws connecting intentional descriptions of reasons and behaviour — is now generally accepted.[16]

In cognitive science the counterpart of the covering law account is what Stich calls the "strong representational theory of mind".[17] Its strongest defender has been Jerry Fodor, who writes that "there are true, contingent generalizations which relate mental state *types* in virtue of their content".[18] But even Fodor seems to have given it up, and in any case Stich offers a number of reasons why he should.[19] Pylyshyn puts the criticism by saying that only physical terms are "projectible" — i.e., figure in genuine laws — and he expresses the prevailing point of view when he writes: "When we say we do something because we desire Goal G or because we believe P, we are attributing causality to a representation, though it is not the content that does the causing.... What actually do the causing are certain physical properties of the representational state...." The reasons for this is, as

---

[16] For the logical connection argument see, for example, my 'Reasons, Causes, and Intentional Explanation' in *Analyse & Kritik* (July, 1986), Sec. III. Davidson's arguments against the covering law account have been much discussed; cf., for example, his 'Mental Events', in *Essays on Actions and Events*, pp. 207–224.

[17] Stich, op. cit., Chap. 7.

[18] *Representations* (Cambridge, Mass.: MIT Press, 1981), p. 26.

[19] Fodor's position on this issue wavers in ways which are confusing; cf. Stich's helpful discussion of Fodor's point of view, esp. on pp. 128 ff. and 187 ff.

he puts it, because "Only the material form of the representation is causally efficacious".[20]

This prevailing mentalist point of view involves an oblique account of causality. According to it, reasons cause behaviour even if there are no causal laws which include either content descriptions of reasons or descriptions under which behaviour is intentional. There need be only *some* description of the reason, and *some* description of the behaviour, connected by causal law, and if only physical terms are projectible (or nomic), these descriptions will have to be *physical.* They will, moreover, be unknown to most agents since they are found, if at all, only in the physical sciences (and usually in their theoretical parts, e.g., in neurology).

Reasons are causes, then, according to this oblique account, not in virtue of their content but in virtue of their (also) being physical — in virtue of their (also) having physical descriptions which are part of a physical law which governs the behaviour for which they are reasons.

I have given in other places what I consider a decisive objection to this point of view, developed most influentially by Davidson, and I shall only summarize the objection.[21]   Grant that agents usually know when their own behaviour is intentional under a description and that they often know that about others. *Given mentalism,* this means that agents usually know when their behaviour and the behaviour of others is *caused* by reasons. The substance of my objection is that such knowledge is not possible under the oblique cause version of mentalism. The argument is as follows.

On the oblique cause version of mentalism an agent's behaviour is caused by reasons only if there is a causal law connecting *physical* descriptions of the agent's reasons and of his behaviour. But it is important to note that this cannot just be a general claim about reasons and behaviour, a claim, for example, that all behaviour is governed by physical laws (something an intentionalist need not deny). For it is by the appeal to causality that mentalism distinguishes an occasion on which an agent has reasons and acts because of them and an occasion on which he has reasons but does not act because of them.

---

[20] Pylyshyn, op. cit., p. 39.

[21] Davidson first stated this point of view in 'Actions, Reasons, and Causes' (1963), now in *Essays on Actions and Events.* See especially pp. 15–17. My objection can be found in 'Oblique Causation and Reasons for Action', *Synthese* 43 (1980), pp. 351–367.

Only on an occasion of the first type do the agent's reasons render his behaviour intentional under a description. Since on the oblique cause version of mentalism all causality involves physical laws, this means that only on an occasion when there is a causal law connecting a physical description of the agent's reasons with a physical description of his behaviour can the agent's behaviour be intentional (under the description given by the agent's reasons). On occasions when there are no such specific causal laws the agent's behaviour may still be governed by physical laws but it will not be intentional.

If the distinction between occasions on which behaviour is intentional and occasions on which it is not is thus to be made in terms of the presence or absence of specific causal laws, then *knowing* when behaviour is intentional and when it is not will require *knowing* when such causal laws are present and when they are not. But we do not in general know when such causal laws are present and when they are not, for they are laws which involve physical (nomic) descriptions of which we are ignorant. In the case of reasons, for example, they will presumably be neurological descriptions, and in the case of behaviour we usually have no idea how to characterize the bodily motions in a law-like way. But being ignorant of the presence or absence of such causal laws, we cannot know when an agent's reasons are the causes of his behaviour and not mere rationalizations of it. For — to repeat — knowing that an agent's behaviour has physical causes is not enough: we must know in each case whether or not his reasons are connected by a physical law with his behaviour, for if they are not, the reasons are mere rationalizations, however rational the behaviour is in the light of them.

Given the oblique cause version of mentalism, then, it follows that unless as agents we have much more physical knowledge than anyone thinks we do, we could only by sheer luck ever believe truly of ourselves, or of others, that we have acted for a reason or that our behaviour is intentional under a description. But since we usually know that of ourselves and often know it of others, the truth of our beliefs is not just a matter of luck.

The only way I can see to meet this objection would be to argue that there are lawlike, or at least reliable, connections between descriptions of reasons as reasons (in terms of their content) and their physical descriptions, connections that are knowable. This reply is not open to Davidson, however, for he explicitly denies that there are any such connections; that is built into his claims that the mental is anomalous and that psychology is autonomous.[22]

Some cognitive scientists have tried to develop this line of reply by defending a version of mentalism Stich calls the "weak representational theory of the mind".[23] Like the strong representational theory it holds that the inner states which cause behaviour have content, but it denies that causal generalizations involve that content. It holds, as Stich puts it, that "the generalizations of cognitive psychology detail the interactions among mental states in terms of their formal properties". But, he continues, "the more interesting version of the weak RTM goes on to claim that the semantic properties of mental state tokens are *correlated with* [my emphasis] their syntactic types" (p. 9). This correlation, it may be argued, is sufficient to meet the kind of objection I have made.

What many advocates of cognitive science claim is distinctive about the field is that it posits a level and kind of explanation Davidson does not deal with, one variously characterized as symbolic, syntactic, functional, or computational. *"The basic assumption of cognitive science"*, writes Pylyshyn, is "that there are ... three distinct, independent levels at which we can find explanatory principles in cognitive psychology" [24] — namely, a physical-nomological level, an intentional level, and a computational level. The point of this third level seems to be, precisely, to show that although no systematic correlations can be established *directly* between the causally impotent intentional level and the causally efficacious physical level, the computational level can link up these disparate levels. It is, one might say, the pineal gland of contemporary mentalism.

Let me quote at some length from Pylyshyn:

> It is not the content that does the causing ... What actually do the causing are certain physical properties of the representational state —

---

[22] Davidson does suggest that certain kinds of common sense (but not lawlike) generalizations hold between physical descriptions of reasons and content descriptions and that this gives us what we need. I argue in my paper cited in the previous note that this will not do.

[23] Stich, op. cit., Chap. 9.

[24] Pylyshyn, op. cit., p. 131. For further discussion of what the computational level involves see Pylyshyn, Chap. 2, or Haugeland's 'Semantic Engines: An Introduction to Mind Design', in *Mind Design* (op. cit.).

but in a way that reflects the representational state's content. There is, if you like, a parallel between the behavioral patterns caused by the physical instantiation of the representational states and the patterns captured by referring to the semantic content of these states. How can this be? How can such a parallel be maintained coherently over time? Only one nonquestion-begging answer to this dilemma has ever been proposed: that what the brain is doing is exactly what computers do when they compute numerical functions; namely, their behavior is caused by the physically instantiated properties of classes of substates that correspond to *symbolic codes.* These codes reflect all the semantic distinctions necessary to make the behavior correspond to the regularities that are stateable in semantic terms. In other words, the codes or symbols are equivalence classes of physical properties which, on one hand, cause the behavior to unfold as it does, and on the other, are the bearers of semantic interpretations (p. 39).

I see two problems in taking the symbolic or computational level as providing the connections needed to meet the objection I have raised to this oblique cause version of mentalism. The first is that if the computational level is to link the physical level with the intentional level, it will have to be linked with each in turn. The link between the physical and the computational level is not problematic; its nature is part of the intellectual achievement which laid the theoretical foundations for computers, an achievement which is significant in showing that scientific connections need not be nomic but can be computational. It is the link between the computational level and the intentional (semantic) level which raises problems. For even if we grant that "symbolic codes" reflect every relevant semantic distinction — so there is a syntactic correlate for every difference in content — these symbolic codes do not determine content. For any syntactic state may have a number of interpretations, and the syntactic level alone — even if we bring in the whole syntactic context — cannot determine which interpretation it shall have — i.e., which content it is "encoding".[25]

About this problem Pylyshyn writes that it is "in general, poorly understood", and ventures to offer only "some extremely modest proposals". These amount to the suggestion that ascriptions of content must be determined by a "principle of global coherence" among descriptions

---

[25] For a helpful discussion of these issues see Haugeland's 'The Nature and Plausibility of Cognitivism' (op. cit.).

of behaviour, including speech, and descriptions of the agent's reasons (p. 40). I think this is true but it is just what Davidson has spelled out in writing "that the cogency of a [rational] explanation rests ... on its ability to discover a coherent pattern in the behaviour of an agent. Coherence here includes the idea of rationality both in the sense that the action to be explained must be reasonable in the light of assigned desires and beliefs, but also in the sense that the assigned desires and beliefs must fit with one another."[26] But as Davidson points out, none of this has anything to do with physical descriptions, either nomological or computational, of what goes on within an agent's body; the coherent pattern to be discovered concerns an agent's behaviour and it concerns her behaviour described intentionally. It is, therefore, with good reason that Davidson has failed to use the computational level to mediate between the physical and the intentional.

The second problem is that, even if there were systematic connections between the physical level of causality and the intentional level of reasons via the computational level, we would not as agents know whether they obtained on a given occasion, and hence we could not know when an agent's reasons are causally idle — simply rationalizations — and when they are causally efficacious, as mentalism requires if they are to explain behaviour or render it intentional.

I think, then, that mentalism faces deep difficulties. The covering law model has been abandoned because we do not have the causal laws it requires. The oblique cause version escapes that difficulty but only by so sundering connections between being a reason and being a cause as to make it impossible to know when anyone acts for a reason.

IV.   Intentionalism

I want now to sketch out an intentionalist alternative to mentalism. Consider this example. Sam parks his car in front of the post office, although it is forbidden to park there that day, and is asked why. Here are some answers he might give: 1) I always park there when I am in the area. 2) The police told me to park there anyway. 3) It's very convenient. 4) I didn't notice the no-parking sign. 5) I forgot it was Friday. 6) I didn't notice the post office.

---

[26] *Inquiries into Truth and Interpretation* (Oxford: Clarendon Press, 1984), p. 159.

Let us consider what can be concluded about the intentionality of Sam's behaviour in each of these cases and how the conclusion is reached. In the last case, "I didn't notice the Post Office", we can infer that Sam did not intentionally park his car in front of the post office, for in this case noticing that one does something is necessary for doing it intentionally. In the other cases, we may conclude that Sam intentionally parked his car in front of the post office, provided each of those answers truly gave his reasons for his behaviour. That he was not lying could be checked fairly easily in the first cases, with difficulty in his saying "I forgot it was Friday" or "I didn't notice the Post Office". While what he said may have been true, however, he may not have given the real reason for his behaviour. Whether or not he did is usually obvious, but not always. Is this an area in which police are generally obeyed? Is he the kind of person who generally does what the police say? Does he pay attention to no-parking signs, as shown by what he has done and by what he goes on to do? Relevant considerations might include things done before the act, things done afterwards, circumstances obtaining at the time, and so on.

Do any of these cases constitute Sam's intentionally parking in a forbidden zone? The case of the police telling him to park there does, since it indicates awareness that it was a forbidden zone. Not noticing the no-parking sign and forgetting it was Friday do not, since they disavow awareness of that fact, and parking in a forbidden zone is intentional only if one is aware that one's behaviour is of that kind. This is not always the case; Sam might, for example, park in front of his house, as he does habitually, hardly aware of it, and yet do so intentionally. Whether he intentionally parked in a forbidden zone remains open in the other cases, since they give reasons for parking in front of the post office, but leave it open whether he had reasons for parking in a forbidden zone. To decide these cases we need to know more about his behaviour, and it may be they cannot be decided.

Intentionalism argues that such reasoning involves principles of practical reason and that these are not causal or empirical but principles mastered in learning the language of action and reasons.[27] Its general thesis is that behaviour is intentional under a description if and only if that description can be linked by principles of practical reason with the

---

[27] For more on these principles see my 'Reasons, Causes, and Intentional Explanation', Sec. IV.

agent's reasons for his behaviour. But it argues that this general thesis is little more than a way of gesturing at the complex considerations illustrated by these examples. The principles of practical reason are diverse, and it may even be misleading to call them "principles".[28] Mentalism is in error in trying to reduce them all to causation: reasons need not cause behaviour in order to account for its intentionality. Even if there are causes of all behaviour, there is no necessary connection between these causes and the intentionality of the behaviour.

Causal factors enter in. The case, for example, where Sam did not notice the no-parking sign, involves such causal factors as why he did not notice it, or how he might have been affected had he done so, but these are not factors which caused his behaviour. The case where he appealed to what the police told him assumes that he heard the police officer, but it need not assume that desires and beliefs were causally active in the mentalist way. Even if there were no particular beliefs causing his behaviour, nor a desire to obey the officer, it remains true that the reason for his behaviour was that the officer told him to park there.

Intentionalism holds that we should take all this at face value and therefore accept the following claims. 1) The distinction between behaviour which is and which is not intentional under a description is to be made in terms of the whole setting of the behaviour, including not only what preceded it or accompanied it, but what came later. There is no single factor which marks out behaviour as intentional, and the concept of intentional behaviour is neither sharply delimited nor always decidable, even in principle.

2) While intentional behaviour is in general behaviour performed for reasons, reasons need not be the beliefs, desires, or other attitudes of individual agents. They may include the regulations of a society, the roles people play, the expectations implicit in social institutions, requests or commands, even when these are not mediated by beliefs and desires which cause behaviour. Reasons need not be internal to an individual; the external setting may itself include reasons for

---

[28] "What practical reason demands," writes Annette Baier, "may have to be specified only as what the wise person would do and advise, whether or not reasons for that advice can be spelled out." 'Rhyme and Reason: Reflection on Davidson's Version of Having Reasons', in *Actions and Events: Perspectives on the Philosophy of Donald Davidson*, ed. by E. LePore and B. P. McLaughlin (Oxford: Basil Blackwell, 1985), p. 117.

behaviour. That is, our environment may *require* descriptions under which it provides reasons for action, and it can provide them
directly, not through the mediation of inner states, whether mental
or computational.[29]

3) Distinguishing when reasons function merely as rationalizations
and when as genuine explanations involves no single factor such as
causation but the diversity of factors already referred to. Sam may
have forgotten it was Friday — when parking in front of the post office
is forbidden — but that may not have been his real reason for parking
there, even though he said it was. Perhaps he would have done so
even if he had remembered it was Friday since he pays no attention
to no-parking signs. That might be easy to determine if we know
how he generally behaves in such situations, or it might be difficult
to determine if his behaviour exhibits no pattern. Sam may be pretty
vague about his own reasons, and inquiry may not so much determine
what his reasons were as fix what they will be in the future. Clarity
about one's reasons is often less a matter of coming to know them and
more a matter of giving them a definiteness they did not previously
have, a definiteness that emerges only in one's future behaviour, which
fixes what one is really committed to and therefore what really governs
one's behaviour. In any case, it is not always possible to distinguish
between rationalization and explanation; there may not be a sharp
distinction, and hence not a distinction in terms of the presence or
absence of a cause.

V. The Assumptions of Mentalism

I come finally to some assumptions of mentalism, assumptions which
are very difficult to shake but which account for the sense that mentalism is the only reasonable alternative to behaviourism. The crucial
ones involve the idea that the only true descriptions of behaviour and

---

[29] A lot is being compressed here. Beliefs and desires are for the most part
internal to an individual, but not necessarily; there may be beliefs and desires
which are irreducibly social. When they are internal to an individual, they may
not be inner states in anything like the sense mentalism conceives of them in
order to construe them as necessary causes of intentional behaviour. All this,
of course, requires more argument. See von Wright's monograph *Freedom and
Determination* and my 'The Causation of Behaviour', *Essays on Wittgenstein in
Honour of G. H. von Wright* (*Acta Philosophica Fennica* 28, 1976), esp. pp. 287 ff.

of the world of behaviour are *physical* so that intentional descriptions are not true of the "external" world or at best true of it only in the derivative sense of describing it "in terms of" causes external to it. This idea has two forms — one epistemological and one ontological.

The epistemological form involves the aforementioned assumption that all observational terms are physical. This implies that observation yields only *physical* descriptions of behaviour or its environment. It implies that we do not, for example, *observe* in any direct way that people say things, or try to do things, or that someone has a reason for behaving in a certain way. We know these things at most by inference from what we do observe — bodily motions or physical stimuli. Terms like "say", or "try", or "reasons", therefore, which are intentional, must apply directly only to inferred states, and these, if we are not behaviourists, must be inner states. If behaviour and its setting are merely physical, the intentional must be inner.

This is one reason cognitive science has such a complex story to tell about the inner processes involved in even the simplest forms of behaviour, or why mentalism insists on the causal role of states of belief and desire even in unreflective and unchosen behaviour. For on this point of view, it is only because inner processes and states are describable in intentional terms that such terms apply anywhere, and inner processes and states must, therefore, bear the entire weight of our understanding of ourselves and our world in anything other than physical terms. This is a picture of the world partitioned between an external world, which, as external, is adequately described entirely by the physical sciences and an internal world of pure thought, their relations mediated by computational processes that are supposed to participate both in the world of physics and of thought. It is in short the picture we know as Cartesian dualism stripped of the complexities Descartes himself recognized.

The grip of this picture on recent philosophy was strengthened as a result of Chomsky's influential critique of behaviourist accounts of language. The way Chomsky divided language into surface structure and deep structure was not philosophically neutral. Surface structure was taken not only to be characterizable in purely syntactical terms — by itself that is a hypothesis worth pursuing — but also to be all we are capable of perceiving directly — and that involves the assumption I am criticizing. For it means that everything else language is has to be attributed to inferred, inner processes. The result is that these inner processes are required to carry a burden so immense that linguistic competence had to be seen as innate to the human species and incapable of being learned.[30]

Intentionalism rejects this picture, holding that both behavioural output and environmental input are normally observed *as* intentional phenomena. We normally take behaviour to be intentional simply on the basis of observation. We observe people looking for a book, setting a meal, trying to open a door, hurrying home. Such descriptions are not normally the result of inference, and when they are, they must be based on observations of behaviour themselves expressed in intentional, not physical, terms.

The same is true for the environmental setting of behaviour. A stop sign is normally perceived not (merely) as a physical object but as a reason for behaving in a certain way. A driver who sees a stop sign and does not grasp its function in the social regulation of behaviour is incapable of normal observation. Stop signs are explanatory reasons for stopping at corners even if there is no causally efficacious desire to conform to what the sign requires. Indeed, desiring to do what the sign requires presupposes the ability to observe that it is a reason which explains why drivers stop at corners.

That these sorts of things are normally observed and not inferred ought not to be controversial. There is controversy because of the assumption that only physical terms are observational, an assumption kept in place by the pull of foundationalist epistemology, which retains its power in philosophy of action. It holds on the one hand that observation must ground judgements in such a way that they are acceptable to anyone regardless of their history, culture, or form of life. What we may rightfully claim to know, it is thought, must rest on a foundation sufficient to resolve disagreement among all inquirers, and any conception of observation must meet this criterion. It holds on the other hand that only physical terms meet the criterion. Intentional terms are inseparable from such considerations as how to assess reasons for action or how to judge the overall coherence of extended descriptions of reasons and behaviour. These are *interpretative* considerations, and they are unlikely to yield judgments acceptable to any inquirer.

---

[30] This is clear, e.g., in Chomsky's *Language and Mind* (New York: Harcourt, Brace, Jovanovich, 1968), Chap. 1.

Physical terms have been framed precisely to avoid such interpretative considerations. It follows from these two points that only physical descriptions will be ascribable directly on the basis of observation.

The intentionalist reply is two-fold. It denies that *any* terms are acceptable regardless of history, culture, or form of life. The attempt to frame terms to escape what I called interpretative considerations has been relatively successful, and such terms are precisely physical terms (in the modern sense of "physical"). But this has required adopting the distinctive point of view Habermas calls "the cognitive interest in technical control over objectified processes",[31] the point of view, namely, of scientific rationality. This allows for universal agreement on the part of all who have been inducted into it, but it remains a point of view, and it is not universal across history, or forms of life.

On the other hand, intentionalism holds that judgments involving interpretative considerations are often observational, for they are often justifiably made without inference. This is simply to admit what is taken for granted in our dealing with each other, namely, that behaviour is normally observed as intentional and that many things in our environment are perceived as reasons for action.

I come now to the ontological form of the mentalist assumption that the only true descriptions of the external world as external involve physical terms. The central idea here is that the ultimate individuals of this world must be physical — that *what* we are describing when we describe behaviour or its setting are *physical* individuals, even if we describe them in intentional terms. We have seen this at work in the way mentalism poses the question about the intentionality of behaviour as "What are the conditions for behaviour, *identified and described physically as bodily movements* also to be intentional under a description?" This forces a causal answer by assuming that bodily movement terms identify *an* individual about which we can ask whether *it* is intentional under a description or what the agent's reasons for doing *it* may have been.[32]

---

[31] J. Habermas, *Knowledge and Human Interests*, trans. by J. Shapiro (London: Heinemann, 1972), p. 309.

[32] The following from Alan Donagan illustrates the way the mentalist assumption works: "The theory of action began with the question, 'In virtue of what are certain bodily movements by human adults human actions and others of the same kind by infants and brute animals not?'... We need an answer... to 'In what did his action

This, however, is not plausible. In parking his car in front of the post office, Sam's body moved in all sorts of ways. His feet moved, his arms and hands turned, his head twisted, his shoulders turned. Considered as bodily movements, these are just a miscellany. But asking whether his behaviour was intentional or what his reasons were, we assume that there is *an* act about which we are asking whether *it* is intentional or what his reasons for doing *it* were. While physical individuation yields a miscellany of movements, intentional individuation yields *an* act about which the question of intentionality or of reasons may be raised. To ask whether behaviour is intentional, therefore, is already to have understood the behaviour in terms of descriptions under which it may be intentional and which may be linked with reasons for action.

It is in this light that we must understand Wittgenstein's famous question: "Let us not forget this: When 'I raise my arm' my arm goes up. And the problem arises: what is left over if I subtract the fact that my arm goes up from the fact that I raise my arm?" [33] Although this passage has been taken as a motto by mentalists, their interpretation is not Wittgenstein's. They interpret it as asking what has to be added to the physical fact of my arm going up to get the intentional fact of my raising my arm. Wittgenstein, however, starts, not with physical descriptions of behaviour, but with intentional descriptions, and poses the question of what we have if we take away the result necessary for the behaviour to be successful. His point is that the concept of intentional behaviour is not a compound of physical concepts plus others, but is a basic concept in that without it we could not identify the behaviour whose intentionality we are concerned with. Our problem is not to specify what has to be added to bodily movements to get intentional behaviour, but to specify in intentional terms the conditions for behaviour — already identified in intentional terms — to be intentional under a description.

It is, therefore, implausible to make the physical individuation of

---

consist?' to which a proper answer would be a description of the movements of his body." ('Philosophical Progress and the Theory of Action', *Proceedings of the American Philosophical Association* 55, 1981, p. 45.) I develop this point about the way mentalists pose the question of the intentionality of behaviour in terms of bodily movements in 'Davidson on Intentional Behavior', *Actions and Events: Perspectives on the Philosophy of Donald Davidson* (op. cit.), pp. 57 ff.

[33] *Philosophical Investigations*, trans. by G. E. M. Anscombe (Oxford: Basil Blackwell, 1953), Part I, para. 621.

behaviour primary and to take *what* we are describing or explaining
to be physical individuals. This does not mean that these individuals
do not have physical descriptions; behaviour obviously does and its
environment can presumably be described in physical terms. But
it is to deny an exclusive or even primary role to physical terms
in individuating behaviour or the setting in which agents act. It
is to argue that the external world itself, insofar as it is an arena
for intentional behaviour, not only cannot be adequately described in
purely physical terms but cannot be understood to include as objects
of description things which are merely physical. Every thing may have
a physical description; it does not follow that it is merely a physical
thing.[34]

What accounts for this assumption that the only true descriptions of
the external world as external are physical and that other descriptions
of it as having meaning and significance apply to it only in virtue of
its (causal) relations to states and events internal to individual minds?
Let me conclude by suggesting two reasons for this.

The first touches on deep issues in philosophy of language. Physical
terms — at least observational ones — carry with them a simple
conception of how language relates to the world: roughly a one-to-
one referential relation of terms and things, with the representational
function of sentences being built on that. It is the kind of picture of
language Wittgenstein worked with in the *Tractatus*. It means, for
example, that physical language is not vague: either a term applies or
it does not, and in principle this can be decided on grounds acceptable
to anyone.

Intentional terms are vague. We are often, for example, in a position
where we cannot say of behaviour either that it is or that it is not
intentional under a description, and there may be even in principle
no universally acceptable resolution of the issue. This is because the
relation of language and world implicit in intentional language is not a
simple referential one, but has the complexities Wittgenstein exhibited
in the *Philosophical Investigations*.

---

[34] Cf. John Dewey in *Logic: The Theory of Inquiry* (New York: Henry Holt &
Company, 1938), p. 42: "The environment in which human beings live, act and
inquire is not simply physical. ... It is cultural as well. ... The occasions in which
a human being responds to things as merely physical in purely physical ways are
comparatively rare."

The implications of this for ontological questions is that such questions present themselves straightforwardly (if at all) for physical terms but not for intentional terms. The result is a bias towards taking physical terms as ontologically basic and intentional terms as at best ontologically derivative — to construe *what* we are describing or explaining, even when we are describing it in intentional terms, as *being* merely physical. Hence the conclusion that the world of behaviour *is* physical, and it has meaning or significance only in virtue of its relation to something else.[35]

The second has to do with the historical setting in which post-medieval science was born. Modern physical science is undoubtedly an intellectual achievement of the highest rank, and that inevitably sets the question of how its mode of inquiry relates to other human practices — to other inquiries, other forms of understanding, other ways of describing the world. One way of understanding that relation got a powerful articulation at the very moment physics entered on the path of a secure science. That way of articulation was Descartes's, who partitioned the world into an outer physical world and an inner mental world. The physical sciences were given the outer world; for its description physical terms were entirely adequate. Everything else was made dependent on the mind, which had to be conceived so as to account for the meaning or significance phenomena have in a world of agents.

This has for a very long time been the dominant way of conceiving the relation of physical science to our understanding of ourselves as agents. It undergirds mentalism, and it inspires cognitive science. It is, moreover, associated with impressive intellectual and technical achievements. But it is neither a necessary condition for these achievements nor the only way of conceiving the relation of phys-

---

[35] Cf. Quine: "It is only our somewhat regimented and sophisticated language of science that has evolved in such a way as really to raise ontological questions. It is an object-oriented idiom. Any idiom purports, more specifically, to tell about objects. Its referential apparatus ... is explicit. ... Ordinary language is only loosely referential, and any ontological accounting makes sense only relative to an appropriate regimentation of language... [This is a matter] of freely creating an ontology-oriented language which can supplant ordinary language in serving some particular purposes that one has in mind." 'Facts of the Matter', in *Essays on the Philosophy of W.V. Quine*, ed. by R. W. Shahan and C. Swoyer (University of Oklahoma Press, 1979), pp. 160, 168.

ical science to other inquiries or to our conception of ourselves as agents.

It is time to explore other ways of understanding the role and status of the physical sciences, ways which admit that the world in which we live and move is not merely a world of physical entities whose meaning and significance depend entirely on the causal role of inner states and events. We as individual agents *find* ourselves in a world of speech rather than mere sound waves, of action rather than mere bodily movements; we do not by the inner workings of our mind bring such a world into being. We as individual agents *observe* persons talking and acting, not merely uttering noises or moving their bodies; we do not know such things by inference. How we are able to observe such things is a puzzling question that must be pursued, but answers to that question should not be confused with answers to the question of *what* is observed. Behaviourism mistakenly assumes that what we observe is merely physical, and mentalism shares that assumption. Because intentionalism reminds us of some truisms about what we do observe of human action, it is a better way of not being a behaviourist.[36]

---

[36] A number of friends have kindly read and made comments on this paper. Lilli Alanen, my commentator at the Åbo Symposium, read more than one draft and helped me in many ways. I have also benefited a great deal from the suggestions of Curtis Brown, Alan Donagan, Stephen Evans, Vicki Harper, John Haugeland, Lars Hertzberg, and Owen Jones.

ON AVOIDING INTERACTIONISM

Response to Frederick Stoutland

LILLI ALANEN

Man need not be degraded to a machine by being denied to be a ghost in a machine. He might, after all, be a sort of animal, namely, a higher mammal. There has yet to be ventured the hazardous leap to the hypothesis that perhaps he is a man. (Gilbert Ryle)[1]

In his paper[2], Fred Stoutland presents intentionalism as an alternative to behaviourism and mentalism considered from the perspective of the philosophy of action. Because of their commitment to physicalism, the latter wrongly assume both that human behaviour can be adequately described in physical terms and that *explanations* of actions require laws connecting external stimuli or (in the case of mentalism) internal events with behaviour described in physical terms.

The point of controversy between the three conceptions of action discussed by Stoutland is the role of intentional terms in action description and explanation. While behaviourists think they ought to be excluded (because of their assumption that behaviour can be adequately described and explained in physical terms *alone*) mentalists, like intentionalists, consider them indispensable. They differ on the question how, precisely, mental or intentional terms enter into the account of human behaviour.

Stoutland's use of "intentional" corresponds to Davidson's use of "mental" or "psychological".[3] Davidson characterizes mental verbs (verbs expressing propositional attitudes) as "psychological verbs as used when they create apparently nonextensional contexts." The distinguishing mark of the mental thus characterized "is not that it is

---

[1] Gilbert Ryle, *The Concept of Mind* (London: Hutchinson, 1949), p. 328.

[2] This volume, pp. 37–60.

[3] Donald Davidson, 'Mental Events' (1970), repr. in D. Davidson, *Essays on Actions and Events* (Oxford: Oxford University Press, 1980), pp. 207–227. Cf. Fred Stoutland, 'Davidson on Intentional Behavior', E. LePore and Brian P. McLaughlin (eds.), *Actions and Events* (Oxford: Basil Blackwell, 1985), pp. 44–59.

private, subjective, or immaterial, but that it exhibits what Brentano called intentionality".[4] The advantage of this criterion according to Davidson is that it makes it possible not only to avoid the difficulties pertaining to a "Cartesian" concept of the mental as identical with thinking in Descartes's wider sense, but also to include intentional actions alongside thoughts and related events in the realm of the mental.[5]

"Physical terms" again are characterized by Stoutland negatively, in contrast to intentional terms in the above sense, as terms not involving "the meaning or significance phenomena have for agents" (intentional attitudes), or "the role or value of phenomena in social, cultural, or historical settings". The distinction between "physical" and "intentional" as made by Stoutland is deliberately vague. Physical terms are said to correspond, roughly, to terms used by the physical sciences since Galileo. Agents, their intentions, the rationality/irrationality of their behaviour are not describable in physical terms in this sense.[6] While Stoutland thinks that the distinction between "mental" or "intentional" and "physical" terms is problematic and ought to be abandoned, he adopts it as part of the current vocabulary in which behaviourists and mentalists state their positions (cf. Stoutland's note 4).

Mentalists assume that any adequate description and account of human behaviour *also* requires the use of intentional terms, and even that intentional terms enter essentially into the description of human behaviour. But they do not think that an account in merely intentional terms is sufficient to explain human behaviour. A full explanation of human action in their sense requires the reasons for action, in the light of which an action is viewed as intentional, to have also caused the action, and that presupposes causal laws. Since an explanation in purely intentional terms does not involve causal laws, which are found only at the physical level, there must be an independent physical description of the action and its causes. Mentalism seems thus committed to the view defended by Davidson who argues that the same event, which *qua* reasons for action is intentionally described, can also be described, *qua* cause, in physical terms, i.e. in terms satisfying a causal explanation in the sense required.[7]

---

[4] Op. cit., p. 211.

[5] Davidson, loc. cit.

[6] This volume, pp. 38 f. Cf. Davidson, op. cit., pp. 210–212.

[7] D. Davidson, 'Actions, Reasons and Causes' (1963), repr. in Davidson, op.

The stumbling block for mentalism is the difficulty incurred in establishing any law-like correspondence between types of events described in intentional terms and types of events described in physical terms. The holistic character of mental term descriptions creates, as Davidson recognizes, an unavoidable "nomological slack" between the mental and the physical.[8]

Much of Stoutland's argument against mentalism turns on this difficulty of relating descriptions in intentional terms to descriptions in physical terms and is derived, essentially, from Davidson himself, who has been one of the most influential proponents of the causal theory of action adopted by mentalists. Stoutland has shown that Davidson's theory of what Stoutland calls "oblique causation" is open to the same kind of criticism as that raised by Davidson against the covering law theory.[9]

The position Davidson argues for is a version of the identity theory known as token identity theory, which denies that there can be strict laws connecting the mental and the physical. Davidson calls it *anomalous monism* by way of contrast with other psycho-physical theories.[10] It is, one could say, a weak form of materialism, which purports to avoid ontological dualism without entailing reduction of any kind (definitional or nomological). The anomalousness (lawlessness) of the mental, Davidson argues, is tied to the holistic and open-ended nature of mental predication.[11] The content or sense and hence the ascription of intentional (propositional) attitudes depend on a vast network or pattern of other propositional attitudes:

---

cit., pp. 3–22. Cf. D.C. Dennett, *Content and Consciousness* (London: Routledge & Kegan Paul, 1969), pp. 34–42.

[8] Davidson (1980), p. 223.

[9] F. Stoutland, 'Oblique Causation and Reasons for Action', *Synthese* 43 (1980), pp. 351–367.

[10] Theories asserting the existence of psycho-physical laws are classified, in Davidson's fourfold scheme, as (a) *nomological monism* (identity-theory materialist) or (b) *nomological dualism* (comprising parallelism, interactionism, and epiphenomenalism). Theories denying the existence of such laws are classified as (c) *anomalous dualism* (Cartesianism, described by Davidson as a combination of ontological dualism with the "general failure of laws correlating the mental and the physical") or (d) *anomalous monism*, which is the position occupied by Davidson. Davidson, op. cit., pp. 213–214.

[11] Op. cit., p. 217.

There is no assigning beliefs to a person one by one on the basis of his verbal behaviour, his choices, or other local signs no matter how plain and evident, for we make sense of particular beliefs only as they cohere with other beliefs, with preferences, with intentions, hopes, fears, expectations, and the rest.[12]

The originality, and also difficulty, of Davidson's position is that it allows for the autonomy of psychology with respect to the physical sciences, without excluding causal (physical) explanations of intentional behaviour. If there are not strict law-like relations between the mental and the physical, and hence is no direct causation of physical events by mental attitudes, the latter, according to Davidson's view, cause the former only obliquely, by the fact that they are also tokens of physical events. The impossibility of stating any strict, scientific, psychological and psycho-physical laws does not exclude a causal analysis of action, because every single mental event is identical with a physical event and the physical events are related in the required law-like manner.

The difficulties of this position have been exposed in several papers by Fred Stoutland and won't be detailed here.[13] Stoutland's critique of Davidson's defence of the causal theory of action gets its particular force from the fact that it uses Davidson's own argument for the anomalousness of the mental, extending it from the level of kinds or types to the level of particulars or tokens.[14] The categorial difference between the mental and the physical emphasized by Davidson rules out not only type identity and hence psycho-physical laws, but also token identity between mental and physical events, and thereby the assumption of oblique causation. John Haugeland has reached similar conclusions in arguing against the token identity materialism defended by Davidson and for a weaker form of supervenience without commitment to any identity between mental and physical tokens. Haugeland argues that individuals or tokens described by true sentences are just as relative to the description level as are the kinds or types into which they are sorted.[15]

---

[12] Op. cit., p. 221.

[13] See Stoutland, (1980) and (1985).

[14] Stoutland writes: "My criticisms imply that this difference between the psychological and the physical should be extended to the level of particulars, and that we should recognize that the psychological not only classifies differently from the psychological but also individuates differently" (1985), p. 59.

[15] "The world does not come metaphysically individuated any more than it

Together Stoutland's and Haugeland's arguments constitute a forceful and persuasive refutation of Davidson's position. In his present paper Stoutland argues that the prevailing mentalist view adopted by cognitivists is also committed to oblique causation and that it is therefore open to the same arguments as those directed against Davidson. If Stoutland is right, his criticism has far-reaching consequences. Before considering the implications of this critique, I shall examine briefly the assumptions of cognitive science and the grounds for thinking that cognitivism faces the same difficulties as the causal theory of action.

The central thesis of mentalism is that behaviour is intentional if and only if it is caused by inner states which are considered the (proper) referents of intentional terms. It is the content (meaning) of these inner states causing the behaviour, which is supposed to provide the reason for the behaviour.[16] According to the currently prevailing psycho-physical model, mental (psychological, intentional) events or states are understood as (at least) token identical with neurological events or states. This is basically Davidson's model. To the question of how the mental event descriptions relate to the neurological descriptions contemporary cognitivism offers an original answer: the relation is to be understood, roughly, in analogy with the way computational events and states of computing machines are related to their silicon substrata: as their functional characterizations. Computational functionalism is the most recent development of the functionalist or causalist view about the nature and role of mental states.[17]

This theory combines a *type* functionalism with a *token* identity theory.[18] Tokens of mental events or states are supposed to be identical with tokens of neurological states, and it does not matter if we cannot identify them, for the physical substratum in which they are realized is

---

comes metaphysically categorized, prior to and independent of any specific description." John Haugeland, 'Weak Supervenience', *American Philosophical Quarterly* 19 (1982), p. 101.

[16] Cf. Stoutland, this volume p. 44.

[17] Functionalism or the "Causal Theory" is supposed to be embedded in what in the philosophy of mind is popularly described as "folk psychology", and it is also taken to capture our "commonsense" intuitions of the mental. Cf. Stephen Stich, *From Folk Psychology to Cognitive Science* (Cambridge, Mass.: MIT Press, 1983), p. 14.

[18] For these terms see D.C. Dennett, *Brainstorms* (Cambridge, Mass.: MIT Press, 1981), Introduction, pp. xiv ff.

irrelevant, as long as they can be identified (as types) at the functional level. This satisfies both the Supervenience condition as defined by Davidson and also the Autonomy-principle: mental states or events are irreducible to neurophysiological states but still supervenient on them. Instead of the two levels of the old "centralist" identity theory few today would be prepared to defend, we have three interrelated levels: the intentional level, the computational level, and the neuro-physiological level. Once mental event or state tokens (occurrences of propositional attitudes) are identified by their functional or causal role in the general programme governing the computational processes of the brain, the question of their relation to the neurological level becomes unproblematic: the computer analogy offers an intelligible and scientifically respectable model of how this interaction can be conceived and realized. It could, roughly, be described as an indirect or oblique interaction.

One cannot but feel sorry that Descartes, who took such pleasure in clear and distinct schemes, did not have access to this ingenious and handy model for figuring out how thoughts can affect bodily movements and *vice versa* or, in contemporary terms, how to get "from motion and matter to content and purpose — and back".[19] Instead, Descartes had to postulate obscure entities as immaterial souls endowed with a mysterious power to direct and be affected by the movements of the "animal spirits" in the pineal gland — something he was forced to admit is inexplicable. Unfortunately for our modern interactionists the new three level model isn't all that clear either, and it is not without reason that Stoutland labels the intervening, computational level the pineal gland of contemporary mentalism.[20]

This new version of mentalism has been described as a weak representational theory of the mind. It holds that the inner states which cause behaviour have content (i.e. are some kind of relational entities) but rejects the assumption of law-like relations between the mental

---

[19] Dennett (1969), p. 40. In Dennett's optimistic view the solution of this problem is already at hand, and hangs (merely) on finding some "... conceptually trustworthy formulations roughly of the form 'physical state S has the significance (or means, or has the content) that p'..." Such formulations can in fact already be applied — at least metaphorically — in describing automatic information processing, where one talks of computers "understanding" directions and messages, "storing the information that p" and so on (loc. cit.).

[20] This volume, p. 48.

states in virtue of their content. Instead, it assumes that nomological generalizations about interactions between mental states disregard their semantic properties and apply to those states only in virtue of their purely formal, syntactic features.[21]

But the underlying functionalistic model is difficult to relate to descriptions of actions in intentional terms. The interesting and problematic assumption here is that whereas the causal interactions between mental states are explained by their syntactic properties, these properties (a subset of "physical" properties) are supposed somehow to "mirror", "reflect" or be "correlated with" their semantic properties — an assumption which, not surprisingly, has proved very difficult to explain and defend. Contrary to what Dennett believed in 1969 it hasn't been that easy to get from motion and matter to content and meaning and back again. Cognitive psychology with its commitment to computational functionalism manifests an increasing unwillingness to talk about contents at all, concentrating all its efforts on the syntactic properties of the computational level, the interactions of which seem so much easier to detail and account for scientifically. Dennett himself has taken shelter (temporarily?) in a mere *instrumentalistic* intentionalism: as long as mental treasures can be purchased with intentionalist coin, we are allowed to use them, ready to give them up as soon as some harder currency is found.[22] Stich urges us to abandon the representational theory of the mind altogether for a purely syntactic theory of the mind. Since there seems to be no way of combining methodological solipsism with mentalism, Stich sets all his hopes on the former for the salvation of (cognitive) psychology as a science. One may of course ask what grounds there are for talking about this future science as a *cognitive* science or a science of the *mind.* But the syntactic approach is at least more cogent than the representationalist one and takes the problems mentalism faces seriously. It faces, however, great difficulties of its own which cannot be discussed here.

I take Stoutland's argument as showing that mentalism, also in its most recent developments, shares assumptions with the causal theory of action which render it vulnerable to the objections raised against

---

[21] Stich, op. cit., pp. 9, 185 ff.

[22] See, e.g., *Brainstorms*, Introd., p. xviii, and 'Three Kinds of Intentional Psychology', in R. A. Healey (ed.), *Reduction, Time and Reality* (Cambridge: Cambridge University Press, 1981).

the causalist position. I therefore agree with him that mentalism does not and indeed cannot constitute a viable alternative to behaviourism. The introduction by cognitivists of a third computational level by no means solves the problem of relating mental or intentional descriptions to physical descriptions, since the relation between the intentional descriptions and the intervening functional descriptions remains as mysterious as ever. Contemporary mentalists like to look back at Cartesian interactionism as a superseded hypothesis which can be justly ridiculed and is safely buried. But one may well ask whether the difficulties they face are not fundamentally of the same kind. The problem today, of course, is set in different terms and discussed mainly as a conceptual or linguistic, not as an ontological, problem. However, as long as mentalists commit themselves to realism and to some form of identity-theory, the old metaphysical problems are bound to turn up in new disguises — sometimes so well disguised that they are mistaken for empirical problems. But on closer scrutiny the anomalous monism defended by Davidson and its recent variants seem to be at least as problematic as the versions of monism or the scandalous anomalous dualism they are supposed to supplant.

Dennett's way of stating the problem is, it seems to me, symptomatic. Having distinguished two levels of explanation (personal and subpersonal), and admitted that the object of explanation is not the same at those two levels, Dennett goes on to ask how the two levels are related, and holds that answering this question is a philosopher's task. The question arises for Dennett because of his commitment to physicalism and realism, and because he thinks the Rylean categories should be construed as different "ontological categories, which is to say: the *terms* are construed to be in different categories and only one category of terms if referential." Because the terms on the personal level, according to Dennett, have no reference, there can be no relation between states or events described in physical terms and states or events described in intentional or mental terms: there just are no distinct mental processes to which the physical processes could be related (e.g., "pain"). The problem, for Dennett, is hence to relate *talk* about the mental, for instance, about pain, to "neural impulses or talk about neural impulses".[23] But this, it seems to me, is to beg the question. Having paid his tribute to Wittgenstein and

---

[23] Dennett (1969), pp. 95–96.

Ryle by recognizing the importance of not confusing the personal and sub-personal levels of explanation, Dennett makes the very category-mistake he thinks one should avoid, for in accepting a version of the "centralist" view he commits himself to a mechanical (instead of the dualist's "paramechanical") hypothesis of the nature and workings of the mind.[24] Philosophy of mind, in this view, becomes a kind of "armchair science": speculations about hypotheses the details and verification of which are left to future empirical neurophysiology.[25]

As Stoutland reminds us, there is a level of explanations which are empirical (in a broader sense than physicalist empiricism requires) without being causal, and which are intentional without being committed to the assumptions of mentalism or methodological solipsism. Action descriptions at this level are couched in intentional terms and are based on observation, but the object of observation here is not merely or primarily bodily movements caused by reactions in the brain to external stimuli. What we observe, directly, are actions executed by real people embedded in various social, cultural and historical contexts which contribute in an essential way to determine the reasons on which they act, and which cannot be disregarded by any account that aims at explaining these actions. True to the spirit of Wittgenstein and Ryle, from whose writings it takes its inspiration, intentionalism ignores the ontological questions altogether and hence remains neutral on the issue of the old -isms, and it also avoids taking any clearcut or fixed distinction between mental and physical terms for granted.

It is not very clear, however, in what sense intentionalism, as presented by Stoutland, can be considered an *alternative* to behaviourism or mentalism, both of which commit themselves to some form of physicalism and to a causal explanation of behaviour.

Intentional explanations are not causal: reasons can explain behaviour without being the causes of behaviour. Indeed they cannot be causes in the required sense because once the token identity thesis is thrown overboard there is no matching between reasons and causes in the sense assumed in strictly scientific causal explanations.[26]

---

[24] Dennett (1969), pp. 39 ff. and 95. Cf. G. Ryle (1949), p. 319.

[25] Dennett (1969), p. 42. Cf. Dennett (1981), p. xiii–xiv.

[26] I think this qualification is important, for I don't believe Stoutland or any intentionalist would deny that reasons can function and be regarded as causes in a more common ordinary language sense. See Georg Henrik von Wright, *Explanation and Understanding* (London: Routledge & Kegan Paul, 1971), p. 95, note 19. Cf.

Reasons are irreducible to causes of behaviour of the kind mentalists and behaviourists seek to establish. But once this is admitted, one may ask whether intentionalists and mentalists can be said to seek answers to the same questions. Behaviourism and mentalism, or at least those developments of mentalism which have been discussed here, seek causal explanations of behaviour which are generalizable not only to the actions of human beings, fullgrown members of a linguistic and social community, but to the behaviour of other living beings (infants and animals) as well, and even of inorganic machines (cognitivism). The generalizations they aim at are supposed to be subsumable under — or at least not incompatible with — the laws of physics. The compatibility with physicalism of explanations in terms of reasons, values and goals is of no concern to the intentionalist, who poses his questions at an altogether different level. At least it ought not to be, if the lesson from Wittgenstein and Ryle is properly understood.

While Dennett stresses the importance of this lesson, he seems not to accept the full implications of the distinction he draws between the personal and the sub-personal level of explanation. Dennett admits that the personal level, in "one important but narrow sense", is the *only* level of explanation where human minds and actions are concerned: in abandoning the personal level we abandon the very subject matter (mental states, events). In the case of pain, for example, we stop talking of pain at the sub-personal level and talk about something else, e.g., "the motions of human bodies or the organization of the nervous system". At the sub-personal level there are no mental events and processes and, it should be added, there are no actions either. In another important sense, Dennett argues, it is however false, although this is "often missed". He writes: "The recognition that there are two levels of explanation gives birth to the burden of relating them", and that, he believes, is a genuine philosopher's task.[27] A similarly ambivalent attitude can be found also in 'Three Kinds of Intentional Psychology' where Dennett recognizes the difference in conceptual and causal enquiries but denies that conceptual and causal answers to conceptual questions are incompatible: conceptual answers to conceptual

---

also the distinction drawn by Haugeland between two senses of cause on which Davidson's argument for token-identity seems to equivocate, Haugeland (1982), Sec. II.

[27] Dennett (1969), p. 95.

questions don't rule out causal answers to the same (!) questions.[28]

What should be recognized is that conceptual or semantic and causal enquiries are not only different but independent of each other, and that they cannot, therefore, be related in the way mentalists assume: they have entirely different subject matters. Stoutland contributes to showing that the explanation model exemplified by recent variants of mentalism (e.g. the "weak" representational theory of mind) is a kind of hybrid resulting from the mixing of conceptual inquiries about intentionality with scientific inquiries about causal mechanisms and that it does not therefore constitute a viable alternative to the behaviourist or neobehaviourist theories it is supposed to replace. The mentalist model is a failure in so far as it tries to combine or relate two different and logically independent frames (or levels) of description. If, as I think Stoutland's and Haugeland's arguments imply, descriptions in intentional terms are independent of descriptions in functionalist or neurophysiological terms — if, i.e., there is no correspondence at all between the particulars or "tokens" individuated by those descriptions — then, indeed, there is no point in trying to relate those descriptions, but also, there is no point in comparing them either. This is also why the idea of replacing intentional idioms by more exact "scientific" descriptions, and indeed, the idea of eliminating intentionalist terms altogether, is so futile: they cannot be eliminated unless we drop the subject matter as well, that is, unless we cease acting and reacting like human beings.

---

[28] Dennett, in R. A. Healey (ed.), (1981), pp. 38 ff.

COSMOLOGICAL EXPLANATION
AND UNDERSTANDING

ANTHONY KENNY

In his book *Explanation and Understanding*[1] G. H. von Wright distinguished between two traditions of scientific inquiry. One of them he called Aristotelian and the other Galilean. The former could be called teleological, or finalistic; the second could be called causal or mechanistic. The latter has been broadly characteristic of the natural sciences, and has as its goal explanation; the former has been characteristic of the historical sciences, or *Geisteswissenschaften,* and has as its goal understanding. Much of von Wright's endeavour is to show where the social and behavioural sciences stand with respect to this dichotomy.

The model of causal explanation from which von Wright starts — though he modifies it considerably — is the covering law model of explanation associated with the name of Hempel.

> Why did E happen? In order to answer the question, we point to certain other events or states of affairs $E_1, \ldots, E_m$ and to one or several general propositions or laws $L_1, \ldots, L_n$ such that the occurrence of E (on the occasion in question) follows logically from those laws and the fact that those other events (states) have occurred (obtain).[2]

The model of teleological explanation from which von Wright starts is the practical syllogism of Aristotle. The starting point or major premise of the syllogism mentions some wanted thing or end of action; the minor premise relates some action to this thing, roughly as a means to an end: the conclusion consists in the use of this means to secure this end. Von Wright says, summarizing:

> Broadly speaking, what the subsumption-theoretic model is to causal explanation and explanation in the natural sciences, the practical syl-

---

[1] G. H. von Wright, *Explanation and Understanding* (London: Routledge & Kegan Paul, 1971).
[2] Op. cit., p. 11.

logism is to teleological explanation and explanation in history and the social sciences.[3]

I think that this insight is correct and profound. I am not concerned with following the application of the insight where von Wright applies it — namely to the sciences of man. I wish instead to investigate whether it has any application at the most fundamental level of making the universe intelligible.

Before doing so, however, I wish to bring out two aspects of the distinction which von Wright mentions, indeed, but which for his purposes he did not need to develop.

First, teleological explanation applies not *only* to the sciences of man. Von Wright says:

> One could divide the domain traditionally claimed for teleology into two subprovinces. One is the domain of the notions of *function, purpose*-(fullness), and *"organic wholes"*.... The other is that of *aiming* and *intentionality*. Function and purpose figure prominently in the biological sciences, intentionality in the behavioral sciences, social study, and historiography.[4]

Secondly, to understand a teleological explanation one has to some extent to share in the goal which figures as the major premise of the practical syllogism. That is not to say that one has to make the good pursued *one's own good*. But one must be able to *see it as a good*. In this way understanding something (in von Wright's sense of understanding) involves valuation in a way in which explanation does not. If you wish to understand someone's action you need not just be able to reconstruct the practical syllogism on which he acts, you need to empathise with the goal he pursues. Otherwise you do *not* understand his behaviour. (Think of cases of vandalism. "Yes, I see that he did what he did because it was the most effective way to wreck the telephone kiosk: but what was the good of doing that? What was in it for him?")

This point is only glancingly alluded to by von Wright, when he connects understanding (*Verstehen*) with empathy (*Einfühlung*), the recreation, that is to say, in the mind of the scholar of the mental atmosphere of the object of his study.

---

[3] Ibid., p. 27.
[4] Ibid., p. 16.

What I want to do in this paper is to ask whether there is any sense in which we can say that either explanation or understanding is more fundamental than its counterpart; and whether either has an application to very general issues such as the origin of life and of the cosmos itself. I am given a stimulus to do so by the very last paragraph of von Wright's book:

> From the relativistic rationalism which views actions in the light of set purposes and cognitive attitudes of agents must be distinguished an absolute rationalism which attributes a goal to history or the social process as a whole. This goal can be thought of as something immanent, as I think we have to understand Hegel's notion of the objective and the absolute mind (*Geist*). Or it can be something transcendental, like various models of world-explanation offered by Christian theology. It can perhaps aim at a combination of both types of view. But all such ideas transcend the boundaries of an empirical study of man and society, and therefore also of anything which could reasonably claim to be a "science" in the broader sense of the German word *Wissenschaft*. They may nevertheless be of great interest and value. A teleological interpretation of history and society can influence men in a variety of ways. An interpretation in terms of immanent or transcendental aims can make us acquiesce in things as they happen, thinking that they serve a purpose unknown to us. Or it can urge us to action for ends purported to be set, not by the contingent wills of individual agents, but by the very nature of things or by the will of God.

All such ideas, he says, transcend the boundaries of an empirical study of man and society, and therefore also of anything which could reasonably claim to be a science in the broadest sense.

I agree with this: but I ask what, then, is this "interest and value" of which von Wright speaks. Is it simply the fact that ideas of teleology in history — like superstition — may have an influence on people and in that way account for their actions? Or can such things have a *cognitive* interest and value?

I note that von Wright has no word to embrace *both* explanation and understanding. I have not been able to find one either. But it seems clear to me that explanation and understanding are two species of a common genus. Earlier, I said that both explanation and understanding are scientific activities, designed to render the world intelligible. The Latin word *"intelligere"* does indeed seem to cover both explanation and understanding, at least as that word was used by the medieval schoolmen. But I know of no simple English word; the concept is perhaps rendered by phrases such as "making sense of" or "rendering intelligible". The German word *"begreifen"*, I am told, may serve the same purpose.

My question is this: if life and the cosmos can be rendered intelligible, or made sense of, then is explanation or understanding the appropriate mode for the enterprise? Is teleological understanding or mechanistic explanation the fundamental level at which scientific exploration should take place? Do the two modes of intelligibility — explanation and understanding — apply not only at the superficial level of biology, but also at the most fundamental level of cosmic intelligibility?

One of the traditional arguments for the existence of God sought to answer this question. The argument from design — whether it took the form of an argument from an alleged cosmic order pervading the universe or, like Aquinas' fifth way, started from particular phenomena in the natural world where we find the skilful adaptation of means to ends in the absence of any natural agent possessing the relevant skill — sought to show that the level of understanding underlay the level of explanation: that at the deepest level of all, mechanistic explanation must give way to teleological understanding. The tension between the two types of approach pervades the history of ancient and modern philosophy.

Socrates, in the *Phaedo,* describes his gradual disillusionment with the mechanistic explanations of natural science. He was pleased when he heard that Anaxagoras had explained everything by *nous* or mind; but he was disappointed by the total absence of reference to value in that philosopher's work. He was like someone who said that all Socrates' actions were performed with his intelligence, and then gave, as a reason why he was sitting here in prison, the constitution of his body from bones and sinews, and the nature and properties of these parts, without mentioning that Socrates judged it better to sit here in obedience to the Athenian court's sentence. "If anyone wants to find out the reason why each thing comes to be or perishes or exists, this is what he must find out about it: how is it best for that thing to exist, or to act or be acted upon in any way?" (*Phaedo* 97d). For Socrates, teleological explanation was deeper, more profound, than mechanistic explanation.

At the opposite extreme from Socrates stood Descartes. "I consider the usual inquiries about final causes to be wholly useless in physics; it could not but be rash for me to investigate the aims of God." Gassendi objected that rejecting final causes meant rejecting the best argument for the existence of God. Descartes was unmoved: a study of the parts of plants and animals might make us praise their maker but would not tell us for what end he acted. The knowledge of a thing's purpose would never tell us its nature: the practice of arguing from ends was Aristotle's greatest fault. God's purposes are hidden from us and it is rash to want to plunge into them.[5] For Descartes it is mechanistic explanation, not teleological, which is fundamental for the philosopher of nature.

Contemporary scientific thought is more sympathetic to Descartes than to Socrates. Jacques Monod attributes to Descartes the discovery of the canon of scientific objectivity.

> The cornerstone of the scientific method is the postulate that nature is objective. In other words, the *systematic* denial that "true" knowledge can be reached by interpreting phenomena in terms of final causes — that is to say, of "purpose".[6]

Modern mechanistic explanations of teleological phenomena are however less austerely mechanistic than Descartes himself would have wished. His aim was to explain all that happens in nature simply by the geometrical properties of matter in motion. The fundamental properties of matter called in aid in modern explanations of the behaviour of living beings go far beyond the sparse apparatus of Cartesian cosmology. But the explanations given are mechanistic in the sense of being explanations in terms of initial conditions and covering laws in whose statement no value-terms appear.

Descartes, it is well known, rejected explanation of gravity in terms of the attraction between bodies, on the grounds that this was a teleological explanation which postulated in inert bodies knowledge of a goal or terminus. But the essence of teleological explanation is not the fact that the explanation is given *ex post*, or by reference to the *terminus ad quem*. It is rather the part played in the explanation by the notion of purpose: the pursuit of good and the avoidance of evil. Nor is it essential to teleological explanation that it should be

---

[5] Descartes, *Fourth Meditation; Fifth Replies; Entretien avec Burman,* n. 29.
[6] J. Monod, *Chance and Necessity* (London: Collins, 1972), p. 30.

regular — or, for that matter, that it should be irregular. Newtonian inertia and Newtonian gravity provide examples of regularities which are not beneficial for the agents which exhibit them. All teleological explanation is in terms of the benefit of agents: but within this there are *ex ante* regularities (like instinctive avoidance behaviour) and *ex post* regularities (like specific habits of nest-building); there are also *ex ante* explanations of non-rule governed behaviour (such as human action out of the motive of revenge) and *ex post* explanations of non-rule governed behaviour (such as the explanation of human action in terms of intention and purposes).

The nature of teleological explanation is often misstated both by its critics and by its defenders. Critics allege that to accept a teleological explanation is to accept backwards causation: the production of a cause by its effect. Whether or not backwards causation is the non-sense it is usually taken to be, teleological explanation does not involve any acceptance of it, as Charles Taylor showed. All that is necessary is that the law covering the behaviour of a teleological agent should be of the form "A will do whatever behaviour B is required in circumstances C to achieve its goal G". What are the standard goals of an agent A, and what behaviour is required in particular circumstances, may be subjects of straightforward empirical inquiry. Someone offering a teleological explanation is not saying that the goal is the efficient cause of the behaviour. On the contrary, the behaviour brings the goal into effect, if it is successful. If it is not successful, the goal never comes into being: if backwards causation was what was in question, we would here have an effect without its cause.

At the other extreme, defenders of teleological explanation have been known to claim that all causal explanation is somehow teleological. Causal laws, it is argued, if they are not to be subject to constant falsification in the real world, must be stated in terms of the tendency of causal agents to produce certain effects. But are not laws stated in terms of tendencies teleological laws, since tendencies are defined in terms of their upshot? Aquinas seems to have argued that since many actions of natural agents are described by verbs which import the bringing about of certain ends (as wetting is bringing it about that something is wet, and cooling is bringing it about that something is cool), all natural agents, and not just living ones, act for the sake of ends. But an act may be defined by its result, and a tendency be specified as a tendency to perform such an act, without this "end" in the sense of final state being an "end" in the sense of goal. Not every result of an action is a goal of that action. A tendency is only teleological if it is a tendency to do something for the benefit of the agent (or of something bearing a special relation to the agent).

In truth, teleological agency is neither universal (as Aquinas maintained) nor mythological (as some modern sceptics have argued). It is above all characteristic of living organisms. Monod says that endowment with a purpose is a fundamental characteristic of all living beings without exception: "the latter are distinct from all other structures or systems present in the universe by this characteristic property, which we shall call teleonomy".[7]

Any teleological explanation must involve an activity which can be done well or badly, or an entity for which there can be good or bad. The paradigm of such entities is the living organism: that has needs, can flourish, can sicken, decay and die. Let us call entities for which there can be good and bad *beneficiaries*. Not only living beings are beneficiaries: so are their parts, artefacts, environments; for them too things can be good or bad. Thus beneficiaries include the organs of animals (eyes, liver etc.); artefacts, such as nests, vehicles, honeycombs, tools; and social institutions such as the family, legal punishment, armies. Numbers, classes, rocks, dust, mud are not beneficiaries: things are not good or bad for them. The theoretical entities of physics, likewise, are not beneficiaries.

Only beneficiaries can have purposes, though not all beneficiaries have purposes. All trees are beneficiaries, like other living things; but an individual tree, in the wild, does not have a purpose (though of course a tree may be planted in a garden for a purpose, such as to shade a particular corner; and if there is a God the existence of trees in general no doubt has its place in some overall plan). But only what has things good or bad for it can have a purpose, and the purposes of those things which are not living organisms are derived from the good or bad of organisms. A thing can have a purpose if it is a part of, or a context for, something which has a good of its own.

There are two ways in which things may have purpose: they may exist to serve a purpose, and they may act for a purpose. The first kind of purpose is function: things which exist for a purpose have

---

[7] Monod, op. cit., p. 20.

that purpose as their function. Thus the organs of animals operate to serve a particular purpose which is their function: they are indeed defined by their function. Thus to describe something as a heart is to refer to the purpose it serves in an organism: that of pumping blood. The circulation of the blood is the function which not only defines the heart, but gives the reason for its existence: that is why animals have hearts, in order to circulate their blood.

The complex organisms within which the organs have their role or function do not themselves, in the same way, have functions. Some of them, such as plants, perhaps do not have purpose at all; but animals have purposes, but not functions. That is to say, their existence does not in the normal case serve a purpose, but they perform many actions with a purpose: spiders weave webs, birds build nests, dogs dig up buried bones.

Having a purpose does not involve, necessarily, knowledge or intention of that purpose. Not all purposes of entities are conscious goals or projects of that entity. The activity of the spider has as its purpose the construction of the web, as the activity of the dog has as its purpose the retrieval of the bone; but the dog is conscious of the purpose of its activity as the spider is not. Not all purposeful actions are intentional actions, and not all entities with purposes are entities that have been designed by those whose needs they serve. Whether or not my liver was designed by God, it was certainly not designed by me.

Purpose, then, is not the same as design. The difference between the two is this. Design is purpose deriving from a conception of the good which fulfils the purpose. Both entities and actions may be designed, though the notion of design is more at home when we are speaking of entities and systems than when we are speaking of actions. When we are speaking of actions it is more natural to speak of them as intentional than to speak of them as designed. But just as purpose in the broad sense includes both the functions of entities and the goals of actions, so design, as purpose deriving from conception of the good, includes both the design of structures and the intentions with which agents act.

What is meant by saying that design is purpose deriving from a conception of the good? A conception of the good may be manifested in representations of it (as in the patterns, blueprints, descriptions and thoughts of human designers) or in expressions of it (as in the display of pleasure in animals). When purpose is design the design may either be immanent to the purposive agent (as with the projects of humans) or imposed from without (as with the function of artefacts).

It is beyond doubt that there are many phenomena in the world which can and should be explained teleologically: such and such happens in order to achieve such and such a purpose. But is such teleological explanation basic, or is it to be reduced to some other kind of explanation? Is the purpose in the world which is neither design immanent to the agent, nor imposed by any terrestrial designer, a basic fact of the world? Or is it something which must be explained by non-terrestrial design, or terrestrial non-purposive agents?

Socrates, having compared mechanistic explanation to its disadvantage with teleological explanation, goes on to introduce what he regards as the safest kind of explanation of all: only by beauty are things beautiful, only by largeness are things large. In addition to mechanistic explanation and teleological explanation, we might say, he commends to us tautological explanation. Corresponding to the three Socratic types of explanation is the threefold Kantian classification of proofs of the existence of God. To tautological explanation corresponds the ontological argument; to mechanistic explanation, the cosmological argument; to teleological, the physico-theological argument. The physico-theological argument, "never to be mentioned without respect", is Kant's version of the Argument from Design. The argument is not nowadays popular, and I want to inquire whether there is anything to be said for it.

It has been pointed out more than once that the argument is ill-named. It is not the step from design to a designer that calls for complicated argument, or meets with much resistance; it is the step from purpose to design. The argument might best be called the argument through design: from purpose, through design, to a designer.

Common to both proponents and critics of the Argument from Design — nowadays at least — is the premise that naked purpose is inconceivable. That is, if we have an explanation in terms of purpose that explanation cannot be a rock-bottom, basic level explanation: it must be reducible either to an explanation in terms of design (intelligent purpose) or to an explanation in mechanistic terms. I shall not question this premise, but it might be questioned, and indeed would have been denied by philosophers as diverse as Aristotle and Bergson.

The question, given this premise, is this. Which is the appropriate basic explanation of purpose: is it design, or chance, or necessity?

Let us start from the cases where our understanding is greatest: human artefacts. If I ask why the room in which I type is at 65 degrees, the answer is that there is a thermostat set to preserve that temperature. That is a teleological explanation: an explanation of the thermostat's behaviour in terms of its function. But of course there is also a mechanistic explanation of how the thermostat works, say in terms of the expansion of metals (which, pace Aquinas, is not teleological). Which of these explanations is more basic? The mechanistic one is more basic in two senses. It operates upon principles of greater generality, which apply to many more things than this particular artefact; and it will explain not only the correct functioning but also the breakdown of the machinery. (If your thermostat breaks down, you send for a mechanic, not a teleologist.) On the other hand, if we ask for an explanation of how the machinery exists at all — which from another point of view is the more basic question — we must seek this once again in teleological terms: the purposes of the designer and manufacturer, and the needs of human beings for a particular environment.

With regard to the artefact, is this the ultimate level of explanation? The answer to be given to this will depend upon one's philosophical view of the explanation of human action. Someone who is a libertarian and an indeterminist will regard the decisions of the human beings involved in the construction of the thermostat as a terminus of explanation. A compatibilist, on the other hand, may have an open mind on the question whether these free decisions and actions may not be susceptible to explanation at a level of greater generality, in the way in which the operation of the thermostat was open to explanation which was, in that sense, more basic. A compatibilist who is also a determinist presumably goes further and believes that at a deeper level than the psychological one there is a mechanistic explanation of the decisions, in terms of some discipline either already existing or yet to be developed.

What of living organisms? Here there are many areas where teleology is involved. Leaving aside the special problems of consciousness and intelligence, there seem to be five principal points at which teleology operates and where teleology must be eliminated if there is to be hope of success in any reductionist program to eliminate purposive explanation in favour of explanation in terms of non-purposive agents. First, there is the operation of mature living organisms; secondly there is the operation of the organs within those organisms. These two phenomena would call for explanation even if every organism came into existence in full maturity as Athena emerged from the head of Zeus. But in fact living individuals develop from embryonic states, and the morphogenesis of the individual is one of the most mysterious of teleonomic phenomena. Fourthly, on the assumption that not all the species now in existence have always been in existence, there is the problem of accounting for the emergence of new species; fifthly and finally, there is the question of the origin of speciation and life itself.

These are five levels at which purpose may seem to call for a designer. One who rejects both transcendent design and naked purpose must reduce the teleological elements here to mechanistic ones. Perhaps the evolution of life is the unfolding of an inevitable process, explained by the natural properties of non-living matter; perhaps it is the result of the operation of necessitating forces upon the outcome of chance occurrences. The latter seems to be the favoured option among contemporary biologists. In his book Monod speaks of "Pure chance, absolutely free but blind, at the very root of the stupendous edifice of evolution: this central concept of modern biology is ... the sole conceivable hypothesis".[8]

With regard to each of the levels of teleology we can raise both the questions: how does it work? why does it exist? But it is clear that the answers to each of these questions at different levels may be related to each other. When we ask of the operation of an individual organ or its parts "How does it work" there may, or may not, be a mechanistic explanation in terms of, say, the stereospecific activities of proteins. In very many cases, no doubt, such an explanation will not be available; but it would be rash to claim that we know that there are some for which a mechanistic explanation is impossible. But even if at this level such an explanation were forthcoming for every teleological phenomenon there would remain the question: how does this system come to exist? The answer to this question, in the case of each individual, will be the story of its generation, its procreation. The procreative cycle is itself something

---

[8] Monod, op. cit., p. 110.

whose existence cries out for explanation; but to explain it is to explain the existence of the species of which it is characteristic. It is thus that a reductive explanation of the existence of species hopes to provide a reductive explanation of the other teleological problems also. The properties of individual organisms, teleonomic as these are, are regarded as given to the individual by membership of a species; whatever the mechanism underlying the development or operation of the individual, the existence of the mechanism is to be explained by the individual's membership of the species; it is created in accordance with the blueprint the individual has inherited from its forbears. The origin of particular species, it is claimed, is explained by the mechanisms of evolutionary pressure and selection. But these mechanisms cannot be used to explain the origin of species as such: they cannot explain the existence of breeding populations, since that is one of the principles of evolutionary explanation. It is the origin of living, reproducing organisms which must be explained, by chance, necessity, or both, if we are to succeed with the reductionist programme.

What is it to explain something by chance? There are two kinds of chance which are explanatory factors. One is the chance which is the unsought outcome of the operation of one or more causes (where more than one cause is in play, this kind of chance is coincidence). The other kind of chance is the tendency of a cause to produce its proper effect n times out of m. The two kinds may be linked together in a particular case: a throw of a double six when dicing is an instance of both kinds of chance. Chance in the second sense is a genuine — if indeterministic — principle of explanation; chance in the first sense is the offshoot of a genuine principle of explanation. There is a third sense of chance — the *a priori* calculus of probability — which is not an explanatory principle at all; its function in relation to explanation is heuristic, to show where an explanation is needed and where none is needed.

Neither kind of explanatory chance necessarily rules out design. A designer may put together two non-conspiring causes in such a way that the outcome is one not sought (pursued, tended towards) by either cause; he may include among the causes indeterministic ones (as a computer programmer may include a randomising element in his program). But if the origin of life can be explained by the chance operation of the properties of non-living matter, then while there may be a designer or architect of the universe, there is no Argument from Design.

It has been argued by Mary Geach[9] that chance could never explain the emergence of a natural power. Chance may bring about an event or action which corresponds to the description of the exercise of a power; but it could not produce it as the exercise of a power. The distinction between actions which are and are not exercises is, I believe, a genuine one. A horse may dam a river (by falling in accidentally); in doing so it is not exercising a power to dam rivers such as the power possessed by beavers.

Correspondingly, Geach argues, though a set of molecules might for-tuitously come into a concatenation corresponding to that of a living organism, it could not fortuitously acquire the power of reproduction. For when we have a reproductive series of organisms, the procreation of each organism is an exercise of a single power, active from case to case. Whereas if the first organism had been the result of chance, then each successive organism in the generative series would be a further, coincidental chance. And this is incredible.

This argument, it seems to me, moves too fast. It is true that if something is F by chance, then it is not the result of the operation of a power to make F. The exercises of natural powers, even the first exercise of a natural power, cannot be something that happens by chance. But does it follow that a natural power could not be acquired by chance?

It seems clear that natural powers can be conferred by art. The powers of man-made fibres appear to be natural powers, even though they are powers of artefacts. (At least they do not seem to be artificial powers in the way that a clock's power to tell the time is an artificial power.) But if art can confer a natural power, why cannot chance? As Aristotle observed, art and chance work in the same field.

We may distinguish between powers and their vehicles. The vehicle of a power is the substance or structure in virtue of which an agent possesses a power (as a round peg has the power of fitting into a round hole in virtue of being round, and whisky has the capacity to intoxicate in virtue of containing alcohol). In so far as a power arises from its vehicle, then chance can confer a power. For certainly chance could cause a certain shape or structure (such as being round); in so far as

---

[9] In an unpublished Cambridge dissertation.

it did so, it would confer the power (e.g. of fitting into a round hole).

If something acquires a natural power by chance, it gets it not through the operation of any natural power: there is no natural or artificial agent whose operation is the production of that power. Is this paradoxical? Is there anything repugnant in the idea that by chance a certain structure is produced and that structure confers a certain power, contingently by the operation of nature?

There is nothing paradoxical here, because there are two different things in question. What is by chance and not by nature, is that such and such a structure comes into being. What is by nature and not by chance is that such and such a structure has such and such powers. The chance event must of course itself be the product of natural powers; but why may not the powers which produce the event be conditional rather than absolute powers: powers to ϕ under certain conditions, rather than absolutely? Thus, for instance, a certain structure may result by chance in the sense that there is no agent which has, absolutely, the power to produce that structure. Thus a certain megamolecule results though there is no molecule which has a power to produce such a structure; but perhaps two molecules each have conditional powers, which are exercised only if they meet another molecule of the appropriate kind, and thus the structure results by the chance which is the coincident operation of non-conspiring causes.

It is not clear to me that it is in any stronger sense than this that the customary story of the origin of life from the primeval soup demands that chance explains the origin of natural powers. Of course the powers that are to be explained if we want to explain the origin of life are powers of a special kind: not just the power to make things F but the power to make things have a power to make things F; what we might call replicative powers. But these do not appear to present special difficulties once we have admitted that natural powers of any kind can be produced by chance.

I confess, however, to feeling residual hesitations about the accounts of the origin of life which I have seen. The difficulties perhaps arise from the popular nature of the expositions which I have read, or betray my own misunderstanding. But it is a common feature of all the accounts which I have read that they fail to make simultaneously plausible two elements which must both be explained if we are to account for the origin of life from the random motion of non-living

molecules. To the extent that the random formation of groupings is
made plausible, to explain the emergence of the first living cells, to the
same extent the account makes less credible the origin of like from like
alone which is the essence of reproduction by breeding. I must leave
it to others to decide whether this is a contingent or necessary feature
of popular accounts of the biological theory of the origin of life.

When we turn from the origin of life to the origin of the universe,
it becomes clear that if there is to be an intelligibility here at all, it
must be of the form of understanding and not of explanation.

Philosophers have held the most diverse views of the role of intelligibility here. Can we prove that the world had a beginning? Can we
prove that the world has continued for ever? Aristotle believed that
one could prove the latter. The Kalam philosophers believed that one
could prove the former. Aquinas believed that one could prove neither.
Kant believed that one could prove both: hence the antimony, which
served to reveal the impotence of reason in this area.

It may be that Kant is right that it is foolish to raise the kinds
of question about the universe as a whole which one can raise about
its parts. But from a philosophical point of view, I prefer the open
agnosticism of Aquinas (philosophy cannot tell us anything here either
way) to the closed agnosticism of Kant (philosophy can show that
nothing can tell us anything here either way). That leaves it open
that cosmologists may be correct when they tell us, extrapolating
backwards from current states and general laws of physics, that there
must have been an origin of the cosmos, a finite period of time ago.

Can we seek any intelligibility here? It is clear that if there is any,
it cannot be of the mode of explanation. There can be no covering law
saying that when certain antecedent conditions hold, then a universe
comes into existence. *Ex hypothesi,* before the universe existed there
were no antecedent conditions in the appropriate sense.

Either the origin of the universe is something completely unintelligible — a possibility which I see no way of ruling out, though I am
unconvinced by Kant's proof of it — or it is to be *understood.* If it
is to be understood it must be in terms of the purpose of some entity
which is not itself part of the material universe. For if the entity in
question were part of that universe it would be part of what needs to
be accounted for. So it must be something not itself part of what is
to be accounted for, and yet capable of providing an account. If it is

not part of what is to be accounted for, it must not itself be changing, nor have a beginning.

If it is to provide understanding, it must be a goal-directed agent. But what goals or value could we have in common with an eternal, changeless being: one which, by definition, has no needs and feels no pleasure? Only one kind of value fulfils these conditions, namely beauty. Beauty depends on no needs; its enjoyment demands no bodily activity, whether the beauty is visual or intellectual. The beauty of the universe is perhaps something which can be appreciated both by creatures like ourselves and a God who, having made the world, could see that it was good.

But: supposing that the explanation of the origin of life by chance and necessity is inadequate. Supposing that the origin of the universe, if it is to be rendered intelligible at all, can only be viewed in the mode of understanding, which involves appreciating the purpose of a purposeful being. The question remains: what do we add to the recognition of the inadequacy of the intelligibility given by the mode of explanation, by appealing to the mode of understanding? What difference does it make if we attribute the purpose to be found in the universe to the design of an intelligent creator?

Descartes was wrong to say that any appeal to final causes involves a claim to know God's arcane designs. On the contrary, when we recognise a teleological phenomenon, we know very well what the purpose is, otherwise we would not have seen the phenomenon as tending to a *telos*. The question is not what the purpose is, but whose it is. Of course, if God has an overarching purpose in creating the universe, this is not solved when we decide that it is his design which enables the eye to focus or the liver to perform its function. But one can offer the argument from design without claiming to do that, and *a fortiori* one can give teleological explanations of natural phenomena without making any such claims.

The difficulty is rather in giving content to the notion of a supernatural mind. Earlier, I said that design was purpose deriving from a conception of the good; and I could illustrate what a conception of the good was by its representation in the case of human beings, and its expression in the case of animals. No similar manifestation of the conception of the good seems to be appropriate in the case of a non-bodily, supernatural, transcendent designer. The conclusion of the argument from design can only be made intelligible if there is some independent account to be given of the coherence of transcendent mind.

It is sometimes said that the argument from design leads to a "God of the gaps": a God invoked merely to fill the gaps left by scientific explanation at any given point in history. If the argument from design is to succeed, the God it points to must be a God of necessary gaps, that is to say, gaps in explanation which can be demonstrated not to be capable of being filled by a particular type of explanation (as, I have claimed, Darwinian explanation cannot explain the origin of true-breeding species). If the argument is to succeed, only necessary gaps in explanation can be invoked: the God of contingent gaps would have only a precarious hold on worship.

SOME REMARKS ON AGENT PERCEPTION

JAKOB MELØE

The drift of what I shall be saying is that we are poor observers of whatever activities we are not ourselves familiar with as agents. This has to do with the way our activities in the world shape our concepts of the world and with the way our concepts of the world shape our perception of it.

Given the strong division of work within each of the countries that the members of this seminar come from, and given the shortness of human life, it follows that we are poor observers of what goes on in most walks of life. My guess is that this is true of each one of us. University teachers do not, as a rule, have a great deal of experience from the diverse areas of working life outside the university. And where we are poor observes, we are also poor agents. What we are then strangers to, or else at home in, I shall construe as a *conceptual space,* or an *activity space.*

I shall sketch a few examples to illustrate these concepts, and the concept of *agent perception.* There will be no more to those concepts than can be worked out from these and similar examples. The two first examples will be drawn from the realm of man-made orderings of man-made objects, the first from *chess,* as a game, and the second from a *kitchen,* as a place of work. The third example will be of a slice of nature, a *rock face.*

My examples are of this form: one person is observing what another person is doing, where the acting person may be either a single agent, acting alone, or one of two agents acting with respect to each other, as in buying and selling. Or my examples are embedded in some example of this form. Some such scenes are: One person working out a proof on the blackboard while a second person is observing the steps. (The second person may be a fellow mathematician or the three year old son of the first.) Two people playing chess and a third looking on. Or a scene like this: I am in a shop, waiting to be served. The customer ahead of me is paying for his goods. He has just been told that it costs

8 Marks altogether. I see him pay with a 50-Mark note and receiving 2 Marks change. Or this: I am in a boatbuilder's yard observing one of the workers clinking a wooden boat. Etc.

In each one of these examples, the agent is also an observer, not of his own actions, but, in the chess example, of the situation on the board. And in the shop example, of the goods that he receives, of the note that he pays with, of the change that he receives in return, etc. (The manner in which these objects enter into the customer's dealings, should be discussed. We should perhaps not make it a conceptual truth that whatever the agent observes is not part of what the agent is doing.)

The character that I call "the observer" is not himself engaged in the activity he observes. That, and that only, is what makes him *an observer* of that activity, whether he is just observing or also engaged in some other activity (which permits his eyes to stray while his hands are working).

But there is this connection between the observer of an agent in action and that same agent, that if the observer is not able to take the place of the agent, then that observer is not a skilled observer of that agent in action. The skilled observer of a fisherman at work is another fisherman. The skilled observer of a surgeon at work is another surgeon. Etc. And these statements should be viewed as conceptual truths, if you agree that we do not master the various concepts of a fisherman's skills, unless we recognize them when we see them (if, for example, we are not able to assess the quality of his manoeuvering the boat while hauling the net). And if you agree that we learn to recognize such skills (to recognize, for example, which practical difficulties (due to wind, current, the slow speed of the boat, etc.) are being mastered, or not mastered well enough) by practising the same art ourselves.

I. The concept of agent perception

There is a lot that a chess player may observe during a game of chess, and the customer in a shop may notice a lot more than that the goods that he receives are what he asked for or that it is a 50-Mark note that he pays with. He may study the general layout of the store or notice the colour of the shop assistant's hair, etc. But when I speak about *agent perception,* or *agent observation,* I speak only of *those observations that guide the agent's operations,* such (operations) as reaching out to receive the goods that is being handed him, and reaching out to receive it where it is being handed him, accepting it as what he asked for, on a short inspection of it, etc. And when the agent is a customer, I treat him as a customer only. That is, whatever he does that does not serve his errand as a customer, is left out. And with those (additional) doings of his left out, we also leave out whatever observations of his that guide those (additional) doings. They are agent observations, but not customer observations.

There is a sense of the word "observe" where it means *let oneself be guided by,* or *abide by,* and that sense should be brought into the sense of "seeing" or "hearing", when it is what the agent is seeing or hearing that we talk about.

Some of the agent's observations I read off from what the agent is saying or doing. If the customer says to the shop assistant, after having received the 2 Marks, "You still owe me 40 Marks", I know that he has observed that it was a 50-mark note that he paid with. If he seems satisfied with the return of 2 Marks, I take it he did not observe that it was not a 10-Mark note that he paid with. When White moves one of her pawns in between her own Queen and Black's Bishop, Black reads off from that move that White has observed that her Queen was being threatened by his own Bishop. And so do I, observing the two of them.

But if Black knows that White is a more practised player than he is, he also knows that the moves White makes may well be guided by observations that go beyond his own, and that he therefore may not be able to read off her observations from her moves. (With chess, it is the skill of the eyes, rather than the skill of the hand, that improves with practice.)

II. To see what there is to see

If White is a lot more practised than Black, then White can take it that she will be able to read off from Black's moves which observations guided them — and which did not (and which of her own observations Black did not make).

That is, White can take it that she is in a position *to see what there is to see* in the moves Black makes. The concept of *what there is to see,* when what is observed is some agent in action, goes together with a concept of the action being *well-defined,* e.g. such that it can be construed as the carrying out of a well-defined instruction that the agent has given himself. Such well-defined instructions can only exist within a conceptual space, or within an activity space, that is itself well-ordered. Well-ordered activity spaces exist, e.g. in some workshops. There, "What did the agent understand himself to be doing?", asked of a skilled craftsman, is a less apt question than "What did he do?". Whether trivial or dramatic, it is such actions that make up the prose of life. And we should study the grammar of prose before we embark upon the grammar of poetry.

Here is an example of seeing what there is to see. Let us say that this is what Black does: he moves his Bishop so as to threaten White's Queen, taking it that White will then move her nearest pawn in between, to protect her Queen, and so vacating a square where Black can then place his Knight. This is the short project of which moving his Bishop to threaten White's Queen is the first step. Now, if White, asked to describe Black's move, describes it as the first step in the two-step project we have just described, then White sees what there is to see in the move Black makes.

III. Not seeing what there is to see

There are two ways of not seeing what there is to see. One is where you locate the action to its proper activity space, but you are not experienced enough, or not (as yet) conceptually equipped, to catch its richness. You don't see enough of it. The other, more dramatic, is where you allocate it to the wrong activity space. You are blind to it.

Let White be a lot less experienced than Black. White may then be too shortsighted to see this one move as the first in a two-move project. She observes that her Queen is now being threatened and that's all. She does not see what there is to see in Black's move. If the very point of that move was to get his Knight into a better position, then that move was essentially the first move in a sequence of two.

In this sense of not seeing what there is to see, we are most of us poor observers of each other's doings — outside our own workshops.

Now let the observer of the game between White and Black be ignorant about chess, even to the existence of the game. But let him also be an experienced fisherman and navigator. He knows his whereabouts, and he observes that the board is oriented roughly 45°

along the 1 to 8 line, so that when a piece is moved parallel to that line and in the direction from 1 to 8, the direction of its movement is 45°. When it is moved along a perpendicular to that line, in the direction from A to H, the direction of its movement is 135°. Etc. He notes that the man moves the black pieces and the woman the white ones. A black piece is now being moved steadily 90°. It travels roughly 20 centimetres. A smaller white piece (the pieces should really be numbered, as fishing boats are) is then moved 45°, roughly 5 centimetres. Etc. He also takes down the direction and distance that a piece travels when it is moved off the board.

This observer does not report on a game of chess. If the form of his reports matches the form of his observations, then he does not see what the players are doing. He is blind to it.

It is not that he makes any false statements. But, as a report about what the two players are doing, his truths are about the wrong objects, the wrong places and the wrong movements. When Black moves his Bishop to threaten White's Queen, that move is not informed either by direction in terms of degrees or by distance in terms of centimetres. The concepts of navigation have no existence within the game of chess.

What is wrong about this observer's reports, is that they construct the wrong space for these objects to travel in. The sequence of moves comes out as just that, a chronologically ordered sequence of otherwise disconnected moves. There is a true report on each move, but between no two such reports can we intelligibly insert a "therefore", "so wisely", etc. To make room for such connections, we must give these pieces their proper space to move in.

IV. Activity spaces

When the fisherman has learnt to play chess, he has also learnt to observe the moves that his opponent makes, and the situations that those moves create. And only then can he take on the position of a non-playing observer and count on seeing what there is to see, or some ordered slice of it.

The game of chess has come alive as a drama, where the pieces have taken on the character of agents, each with a well-defined set of basic actions. The space of chess is a fictional space, where the fiction is that of a feudal battle, where you win if you capture your antagonist's King. The concepts of navigation do not attach to this fiction. What is wrong about reporting that Black moves his Rook straight North-East, is not the misrepresentation of what Black is now doing that stems from Black's *not knowing* that he moves the Rook straight North-East. If it is the fisherman that plays Black, he may well know. What is wrong is that the concept of the direction North-East has no existence in chess. There is no place for it within that conceptual space.

We may speak of chess as a conceptual space, or as an activity space. Within that space the pieces take on the character of agents, the moves take on the character of actions, and the squares take on the character of positions (from where to act).

The objects that belong to an activity space are defined by the activities constituting that space. The Queen is defined by what she can do in the battle, and her colour tells us whose Queen she is. But she is not made of oak, as distinct from pinewood or copper. She is not 10 centimetres tall, or 11 or 12, not within that space. There is no action defined for her in terms of such measurements.

Within chess, there is no description of a situation, and no perception of a situation, that is not in terms of the chess-action it asks for, or invites, or warns against, or in terms of the chess-actions it opens up for or rules out.

White's Queen is *being threatened* by Black's Bishop. That is a perception of a situation in chess, or a description of it. And that *situation invites* White *to protect* her Queen. Black's Bishop is 18 centimetres away from White's Queen, as measured from top center to top center. Even if that description is true, it does not invite any chess action. But then that description, or that perception, has no existence within chess.

And that ends the chess example. The point of that exercise is to sketch a model activity space.

I shall now sketch two other examples of activity spaces. But I shall not try to work them so as to match each point in the chess example. I leave that as an exercise.

Buying and selling can be construed as an activity space of its own, or buying and selling within a particular culture can. A net fishing boat in operation, with a particular technology and perhaps within a particular economy, defines an activity space of its own. And so does a kitchen of a particular make, that is, the kitchen with its complement.

V. The kitchen

The order there is to the objects in the kitchen, the pans and the cauldrons, the plates and the glasses, the utensils, the chairs and the table and the work bench, etc., exists as that order only as viewed from within the activities of that kitchen. Imagine those activities removed, and there is no particular order to it — since there is then no particular point to any of its objects. The glasses in the cupboard are not placed there upside-down, because a glass no longer has any particular orientation. The frying pan has preserved its geometrical shape, but lost its handle. The chairs have preserved their shapes, but lost their backs, their seats and their legs. The stool at the workbench is no more connected to the bench than to any cup in the cupboard, and it is of no particular orientation. Etc.

My guess is that most of us, the philosophers in this room, do not see much of what there is to see in a kitchen. My guess is also that most of us have no experience of not seeing what there is to see there. (Being able to pick out separately movable objects to inspect their colour and geometrical shape, does not count for much when it comes to seeing what there is to see.) But if we have laid the table and washed the dishes, we are not completely blind to its objects and their order.

Not seeing and not knowing that we are not seeing (what there is to see) is a kind of non-existence. If I am blind to chess or mathematics, chess and mathematics do not exist in my world. And so I do not exist in that world where chess and mathematics exist. (It is a terrible thought, and more so for more humdrum examples.)

If we are blind to the objects in the kitchen, and to the various materials in it, such as what is in the flour bags, the syrup boxes, the margarine packages, etc., we are blind to the activities that involve these objects and materials. Seeing that some of these objects are being handled and moved around does not count for much when it comes to seeing what there is to see of the activities of the kitchen. "He is making bread" isn't much of an observation either, if that is all I see. It doesn't touch the art of breadmaking.

The kitchen is a man-made structure. Its objects and their arrangement have been made to fit our activities in it. And so, perhaps, it comes as no surprise that we should perceive those objects in terms of our activities in it.

But what about unworked nature?

VI. The rock face

As a student I practised some rock climbing on a particular rock West of Oslo. When a novice was brought to that rock, I was surprised to notice how little he saw of what there was to see on the rock face.

The rock climber sees the rock face in terms of routes. A route is made up of fingerholds and footholds, distributed in a manner that fits the human body, from the bottom of the rock face to its top. And here, that something is a *good fingerhold* means two things: it means that it is well fitted for your fingers to hold on to and also that it lies within a possible route. What is a possible route is determined by the operative shape and size of the human body and by the climber's climbing-technique. Something isn't a good fingerhold if there isn't a good foothold in the neighbourhood, somewhere beneath. Where it has to be and what it has to look like to be a good foothold again depends on the human body and the climbing-technique.

That is, the description of the terrain in which we move must be made in terms of the possibilities of movement that it offers — if the description of the terrain is to make our movements in it intelligible. For the one who moves in a terrain, his eyes guide his feet, and they do so because he perceives the terrain in terms of how to move in it. And that is how the observer of his movements must see the terrain as well, if he is to make good sense of what he sees.

WHO IS MY NEIGHBOUR?

PETER WINCH

Philosophical discussion needs well-formulated examples; and I want to introduce my subject with a very well known example from the New Testament: the parable of the Good Samaritan. I will give myself the pleasure of quoting from the King James Version:

> And, behold, a certain lawyer stood up, and tempted him, saying, Master, what shall I do to inherit eternal life?
> He said unto him, What is written in the law? how readest thou?
> And he answering said, Thou shalt love the Lord thy God with all thy heart, and with all thy soul, and with all thy strength, and with all thy mind; and thy neighbour as thyself.
> And he said unto him, Thou hast answered right: this do, and thou shalt live.
> But he, willing to justify himself, said unto Jesus, And who is my neighbour?
> And Jesus answering said, A certain man went down from Jerusalem to Jericho, and fell among thieves, which stripped him of his raiment, and wounded him, and departed, leaving him half dead. And by chance there came down a certain priest that way: and when he saw him, he passed by on the other side.
> And likewise a Levite, when he was at the place, came and looked on him, and passed by on the other side.
> But a certain Samaritan, as he journeyed, came where he was: and when he saw him, he had compassion on him,
> And went to him, and bound up his wounds, pouring in oil and wine, and set him on his own beast, and brought him to an inn, and took care of him.
> And on the morrow when he departed, he took out two pence, and gave them to the host, and said unto him, Take care of him; and whatsoever thou spendest more, when I come again, I will repay thee.
> Which now of these three, thinkest thou, was neighbour unto him that fell among the thieves?
> And he said, He that shewed mercy on him. Then said Jesus unto him, Go and do thou likewise. (Luke, 10, 25–37)

The structure of this parable is remarkable. It starts with a request for practical advice. ("What shall I do to inherit eternal life?") The law is appealed to and supplies an answer in the form of a prescription. And this is met with a theoretical, perhaps even linguistic, question concerning the meaning of one of the terms in the prescription ("my neighbour"). So far there is nothing to cause us to raise our eyebrows. But look what happens next. Instead of answering with a definition or a set of criteria, Jesus *tells a story.* Nor does he extract a definition or a criterion from the story but instead confronts his interlocutor with a further counter-question concerning the story itself. When this is answered, he simply *gives an injunction.* ("Go and do thou likewise.") End of episode. What is going on here?

In preparation for answering this I want to notice some further interesting features of the parable: features of a linguistic nature.

The lawyer's question contains an indexical — I mean the first person possessive pronoun "my"; and, correspondingly, the word "neighbour" is *relational.* "Neighbour" in this context might be rendered as *"fellow* human being". The question is not the impersonal "What is a human being?", but something like: "How do I recognize someone else as my fellow?". This corresponds to the fact that the law which gives rise to the question ("Thou shalt love thy neighbour as thyself") although it is clearly to be taken as applicable to all human beings, is couched in the second person singular: it is addressed, that is, to the particular individual who hears it. Hence the importance of the indexical in the ensuing discussion of the law's interpretation. Any one familiar with Kierkegaard's writings on the relation between religion and philosophy will recognize one of his central themes here. The lawyer, like the philosophers whom Kierkegaard so witheringly attacked, obviously expected an answer in terms of some general defining characteristics of the sorts of beings who constitute fellow human beings. Jesus, in responding to him with a story about the relations between two individuals, obliquely conveys to him that his question is not one that can be answered in that way. And the content of the story emphasizes the same point. It is narrated in the process of answering a question apparently concerning the criteria by which I should recognize my neighbour; one might, therefore, expect it to contain some account of the Samaritan's criteria. But it is very pointedly silent about that: "and when he saw him he had compassion on him, and went to him, and bound up his wounds, pouring in oil and wine, and set him on his own beast, and brought him to an inn, and took care of him." Nothing intervenes between the Samaritan's taking in the situation and his compassionate reaction; nor can we ignore the contrast in this respect with the priest and the Levite, especially the latter, who went over and looked at him in a calculating way before passing by on the other side. The contrast is all the more striking, of course, given that the encounter is between a Samaritan and a Jew (as it were a Palestinian Arab and an Israeli): that is, just the sort of situation in which one might expect questions and hesitations.

What is more, once the story is over Jesus does not invite the lawyer himself to extract from the incident the criteria which might be presumed to have implicitly informed the Samaritan's recognition of the traveller as his neighbour. His question is at first sight a curious one: "Which now of these three, thinkest thou, was neighbour unto him that fell among the thieves?" I call it curious because the *original* question seemed to be about who was the *Samaritan's* neighbour (and perhaps how the Samaritan recognized him as such, though I have now eliminated that interpretation). But now the question is who was neighbour to the man who fell among thieves. Has the subject been changed? No, of course not. The point, first of all, is that the relation is a reciprocal one. Thus, *recognizing another as a fellow human being* is in a certain way inseparable from *behaving towards him as a fellow human being*. What the connection precisely is between these notions is the real subject of this paper. But it is in virtue of the connection that it is possible for Jesus to answer the lawyer's theoretical-sounding question with a practical injunction.

I want to make another point about the conclusion of the incident as recounted by Luke. Jesus does not *tell* the lawyer which of those who encountered the wounded traveller was his neighbour; he *asks* him. I believe that this is more than just an effective rhetorical device; just as when, in Plato's dialogue *Meno*, Socrates introduces the slave boy to Pythagoras' Theorem not by *telling* him the answer to the problem but by *eliciting* the answer from him, *that* is not just a rhetorical device either. The suggestion in both cases is that each of us has within him or herself the resources for answering the question: a point which Plato expressed picturesquely in terms of "recollection". The further suggestion is that, in both cases, no one truly *has* the answer who has not arrived at it for him or herself. If the lawyer had needed to be *told* the answer to Jesus's last question he would have been in no position to understand it.

Answering the question "Who is my neighbour?", or: "Who was neighbour to the wounded man?", has to take the form of a practical response. It "has to" because anything arrived at in another way would not be an answer to the question. In fact I should say that the lawyer — and also those of us who feel that his answer to Jesus's final question is the only possible one — are making a response analogous to that of the Samaritan himself. It is tempting to say that we are all responding to the same thing: to whatever it is that falls under the concept "fellow human being"; but this, though it is not wrong, misleadingly suggests that we have some access to this otherwise than through such responses. Whereas what we have to do, I think, is to describe the character of the response itself more helpfully.

The Samaritan responds to what he sees as a *necessity* generated by the presence of the injured man. What I mean by introducing this word can be brought out by considering what someone in the Samaritan's position, and responding as he did, might say if urged by a companion to hurry on so as not to miss his important appointment. "But I *can't* just leave him here to die". The word "can't", as used in such a context, expresses the kind of necessity — in this case an impossibility — I have in mind.

I know that some will be inclined at this point to say that the words I have put into the Samaritan's mouth cannot be "literally" true, since there is no relevant difference between him and the priest and the Levite who, after all, did not even find it difficult, let alone impossible, to pass by on the other side. How then can what is possible for them be impossible for him? The objection would be misconceived, however, since there is a relevant difference: the Samaritan *sees* an impossibility here and the others do not. *That* is the difference.

Of course, that was not what the objector meant by a "relevant" difference. He was thinking perhaps of something like a broken leg, or paralysis, of a sort which would prevent the Samaritan from moving away. But it is clear enough on reflection that this would, on the contrary, be an *ir*relevant difference. This can be brought out if we imagine a bit more conversation. When he says: "I can't just leave him here to die", his companion retorts "Of course you can, you don't have a broken leg, do you?" He would not be meeting the Samaritan's point, so much as making a black, tasteless joke. And the "joke", such as it is, would derive precisely from the *irrelevance* of that notion of impossibility in this context.

But our reflection on the point has not been uninstructive. It has brought out an important peculiarity of the concept of impossibility or necessity we are dealing with here: it demonstrates a difficulty, and perhaps suggests the impossibility, of giving any account of it in "naturalistic" terms.

An example of what I mean when I speak of "an account in naturalistic terms" would be the following. Suppose that *this* time France and Britain really do build a tunnel under the English Channel. (Outlandish examples are a convention in philosophy.) Engineers might determine that, at a certain point, it is *necessary* to excavate at a greater depth than originally planned because of what they have discovered about the rock and soil composition of the sea-bed at that point. That is to say, the necessity of a course of action is here derived from an independent determination of the properties of something. An example from human relations would be the following. In George Eliot's great novel *Middlemarch* Dr Lydgate finds it impossible to oppose the banker Bulstrode's policies for the community hospital because of the control Bulstrode exercises over Lydgate's financial affairs. In both these examples the necessity or impossibility of a certain course of action is supported by reference to probable *consequences*. This is characteristic of such cases; but more central to my present concerns is the fact that in these cases necessities and impossibilities are supported by reference to characteristics of the elements affected by the proposed action: characteristics which can be determined independently of reference to these and similar necessities. A proposed action, or range of actions, is no longer a possible choice for a prospective agent because environmental conditions make the desired end impossible of attainment or generate further consequences which are unacceptable.

A naturalistic account of moral necessities, then, would be one which treated them as limits on the possibilities of an agent's achieving ends which, either as a particular individual or, at the other extreme, as a member of the human race, he is presumed to have. Roughly speaking, this is to treat such modalities as imposing limits not on what someone may *will,* but on what the will is capable of *carrying into effect,* given its presumed fundamental motivation. Such a way of thinking is characteristic of a trend in moral philosophy which has certainly been extremely influential, and perhaps dominant, in the latter part of this century. One proponent of it was Professor Elizabeth Anscombe in a seminal article entitled 'Modern Moral Philosophy', first published in 1958,[1] the reverberations of which have continued through the influential writings of Philippa Foot and broken forth with a considerable augmentation of decibels in Alasdair MacIntyre's recent book *After Virtue,*[2] the whole structure of which is provided by the main point in Miss Anscombe's article. It is the idea, as Miss Anscombe expressed it in 1958, that moral philosophy must wait on "an adequate philosophy of psychology": by which she certainly meant a psychology which would account for practical human rationality in terms of the adaptation of means to human ends. Behind this, I think, was the thought that human ends are derivative from human needs; and behind this again the thought that human needs flow from the kind of being a human being is. In other words the conception as a whole is that morality is somehow based on and perhaps derivable from (an independently graspable) human nature.

That phrase "independently graspable" marks where the difficulty lies.

Let me return to the parable. I emphasized that the Samaritan is depicted as reacting with compassion without asking any questions (beyond those involved in ascertaining the need for help and the nature of the help needed, of course). He does not ask whether the wounded traveller is a proper object of his compassion. This indeed is essential to the *purity* of the compassion which the parable depicts. It is a reaction expressing the Samaritan's conviction that it was *necessary* to help the traveller, that *nothing else was possible* in the circumstances. Now if I put the matter that way, someone may object that I am representing the so-called "necessity" of helping as completely *arbitrary* and therefore no genuine necessity at all. Indeed this is, I think, pretty much the same thought as Miss Anscombe expressed in 1958 when she claimed that a so-called unconditional moral "ought" (of

---

[1] G. E. M. Anscombe, *Collected Philosophical Papers* (Oxford: Basil Blackwell, 1981), Vol. III.

[2] A. MacIntyre, *After Virtue* (2nd ed., London: Duckworth, 1985).

the sort which Kant discussed) is really unintelligible. And Alasdair MacIntyre feels the same about contemporary morality as a whole: its demands are arbitrary and therefore unintelligible.

Miss Anscombe's argument rested on the claim that such a use derives from the notion of being "obliged", "required", "bound" etc. *by law*. According to her the historical explanation for this state of affairs was that a Judaeo-Christian "law conception of ethics" had originally made it intelligible (the intelligibility deriving presumably from a human need — however understood — to fulfil the will of such a law-giver). But, she continued, the usage had lagged behind the disappearance of any general acceptance of ethics as required by a divine law-giver. The situation, she claimed, "was the interesting one of the survival of a concept outside the framework of thought that made it a really intelligible one".

I am not competent to discuss this bold (and unsubstantiated) historical thesis. Let us accept it for the sake of argument. But I do want to question her philosophical conclusion about the alleged unintelligibility of this use of moral modalities in present-day circumstances.

A preliminary point: It clearly does not *follow* from the alleged disappearance of circumstances which once gave a certain intelligibility to a linguistic usage that such a usage now has *no* intelligibility. The most we can conclude is that it now has to be understood rather *differently*. Whether it means anything, and if so what, can only be determined by an examination of its present use — something we do not find in that early Anscombe article.

As a step in the direction of supplying this deficiency let us examine the Samaritan's use of the word "cannot" in my slight addition to the parable. Now it might be thought that this use would fit peculiarly well Miss Anscombe's conjecture about the dependence of such absolute modalities on a law conception of ethics. After all, Jesus tells the parable precisely in a discussion about "what is written in the law" and we may suppose his auditors to have had a conception of God as law-giver. But his parable did not *appeal* to the conception; it *challenged* it. Or at least it commented on the conception in a way which presupposed that the moral modality to which the Samaritan responded would have a force for the parable's hearers *independently* of their commitment to any particular theological belief. It is the lawyer's own response to that modality which enables him to answer Jesus's final question and thus to expand his comprehension of the law. So his understanding of and response to the modality cannot itself be thought of as dependent on his conception of the law. And I might add that it is perfectly possible for *us* to understand and respond to that modality whether or not we have a conception of God as the author of a moral law. Otherwise the parable would mean nothing to someone who did not share that conception — something which is not only untrue, but which would radically thwart one of Jesus's apparent intentions in teaching in this way, by parable.

I should like to go a bit further: in a direction that will anticipate my subsequent argument. According to Miss Anscombe, the intelligibility of the obligation to help the injured traveller to which the Samaritan responded depends on accepting that it is a divine law that one should act thus. I think on the contrary that the concept of a divine law can itself only develop on the basis of our response to such modalities. What I mean can be elucidated by noticing first that in another New Testament context[3] Jesus says of the Commandment which the Samaritan parable elucidates that it is "like unto" another which precedes it: "Thou shalt love the Lord thy God with all thy heart, with all thy mind and with all thy soul." The second Commandment might indeed be regarded as an application, or even a particularly central case, of the first. That is supported by remarks like St John's: "If a man say, I love God, and hateth his brother, he is a liar: for he that loveth not his brother whom he hath seen, how can he love God whom he hath not seen?"[4] The suggestion here, as it seems to me, is that we do not first have a conception of God on the basis of which we form our conception of the Commandment to love our neighbour. On the contrary the conceptual development goes the other way. The responses to moral modalities that we share with the Samaritan (however much they are modified or stifled by circumstance) are amongst the seeds from which, in some people, grows the conception of divinity and its laws. Of course, our understanding need not develop in this direction at all; and if it does not, I do not see why this should stand in the way of someone's grasping the force of such a modal expression in its original context.

---

[3] Matthew, 22: 39.
[4] 1 John, 4: 20.

I do not want to spend too long talking about Professor Anscombe, partly because this is not the right occasion for that and partly because what I have to say about this is being published elsewhere. But I do need to refer to a remarkable fact about the direction taken by some of her later work: remarkable because it seems to me to undermine her earlier views about the moral "ought" but without explicit recognition on her part that this is so. In two papers published twenty years after 'Modern Moral Philosophy' Miss Anscombe discusses certain problems about the use of modal concepts like *must, cannot, ought,* identifying Hume as the philosopher who first brought these problems to light.[5] Hume, in a famous section of his *Treatise of Human Nature,* had worried over the source of the obligation to keep a promise. How, he asked, can the mere utterance of the words "I promise" create an obligation, or a necessity, which did not exist before, of conducting oneself in a certain way in the future. There is no "act of mind" corresponding to these words which could do the trick, and to suppose that the words could achieve it all by themselves seems a magical conception.

Miss Anscombe's suggestion is that this case belongs to a class of modal expressions which she colourfully labels "stopping modals". Children, while learning the language, are actually prevented by adults from doing certain things and are at the same time told "You can't do that" and perhaps given a reason, such as "It belongs to someone else", or "It's her private room", or "You promised not to", or "It's none of your business". Children trained like this subsequently come to respond to the words themselves without the physical prevention which was part of the learning process; and they come themselves to use such words, both in what they say to others and also in their own deliberations about what to do. The reason which is offered in support of such a "stopping modal" is called by Miss Anscombe its *"logos"* and it has the peculiarity of being intelligible only to someone who has already acquired the appropriate response to the cluster of modals which the logos is used to "justify". Professor Anscombe further makes an observation, important both in itself and more particularly in relation to what I am discussing here, that similar considerations spread right through human life, and are involved in the learning of

---

[5] 'Rules, Rights and Promises' and 'On the Source of the Authority of the State', *Collected Philosophical Papers,* Vol. III.

any sort of language; involved in the idea for instance that there are certain things you "can't" say and certain things you are committed to (that you "must" acknowledge) given that you have accepted certain other things. A particularly striking example is the grasp of simple arithmetical concepts of number, addition, subtraction etc. When a child learns to count, it has to be trained, first of all, in a very strict, rigid drill; it has to learn the series of numerals, the *ordering* of which of course is all-important and is, moreover, at least from the point of view of the learner, entirely arbitrary. Again, the disciplines involved in counting objects of various kinds — what sort of "correlation" is required between numeral and object, etc. — has a similarly strict and arbitrary character. Unless a child responds appropriately to such training and goes along unquestioningly with it, concepts of number will never be properly learnt. As I said, that is a particularly striking example, but it is an example of something that runs right through language learning, which involves rote training in procedures to a far greater extent than we may at first appreciate.

It would be wrong, however, to dwell too exclusively on the fact that such procedures have to be *learned:* wrong, anyway, if it distracts our attention from the indispensable role of quite spontaneous reactions on our part in circumstances of different sorts. Indeed, if such characteristic reactions were not the norm, the sort of learning I have referred to would be impossible, since training in procedures relies for its success on the predictability of responses to such training. Not all those responses can themselves be products of training; to suppose so would be to involve oneself in an infinite regress. It seems to me that failure to take account of this spontaneity is a gap in Miss Anscombe's account of "stopping modals" and one which perhaps hinders her from pushing her argument as far as it will go.

I want to concentrate on the application of these ideas to our understanding of each other. Miss Anscombe, as I have said, emphasizes the importance of the fact that in our acquisition of concepts which form what she calls the *"logoi"* of the modals we respect in our dealings with each other, we are actually prevented by our teachers from doing certain things in various kinds of circumstances. I want to add that it is an important fact about us that our reactions to each other are in all sorts of ways quite different from our reactions to anything else. In the present context its importance lies in its connection with our understanding of the kinds of creature we are having commerce with. If for instance I see another person accidentally strike his thumb a heavy blow with a hammer, I will wince, cry out and clutch my own thumb. I have not learned to do this; neither do I do it as a result of reflection on the pain my companion is in. It is itself *an expression* of my recognition of the pain he is in.

And consider the following (wonderful, I think) passage from Wittgenstein's discussion of the relation between mind and body:

> But isn't it absurd to say of a *body* that it has pain? And why does one feel an absurdity in that? In what sense is it true that my hand does not feel pain, but I in my hand?
>
> What sort of issue is: Is it the *body* that feels pain? — How is it to be decided? What makes it plausible to say that it is *not* the body? — Well, something like this: if someone has a pain in his hand, then the hand does not say so (unless it writes it) and one does not comfort the hand, but the sufferer: one looks into his face.
>
> How am I filled with pity *for this man?* How does it come out what the object of my pity is? (Pity, one may say, is a form of conviction that someone else is in pain.)[6]

Wittgenstein characterizes such observations as this as "remarks on the natural history of mankind". His point is that thought and understanding have to be looked at in a "natural historical way": as concepts characterizing the kinds of life lived by human beings. If one looks at things in that way it will seem more than natural that the understanding human beings have *of each other* should be a function of the lives they lead.

Jonathan Swift was a writer whose peculiar sensitivities reflect very well what is involved in this thought. I am thinking both of the chilling 'A Modest Proposal' and the (in a way equally chilling) 'Voyage to the Houyhnhnms' in *Gulliver's Travels.* Out of respect for the squeamish I will refrain from discussing the former at length. I will simply note that the effectiveness of Swift's savage satire on the bureaucratic mind is almost entirely due to the way in which his proposal, and his way of presenting it, completely short-circuit our shared humanity with the wretched Irish peasantry and their offspring. This could serve as a starting point for reflection on the nature of the *bafflement* and

---

[6] *Philosophical Investigations,* Part I (Oxford: Basil Blackwell, 1953), paras 286–7.

incomprehension, as well as horror, we feel in the face of such a phenomenon as the Holocaust in Nazi Germany. I feel like saying that it is important to recognize that here there is something which in a certain sense is not to be "understood", if we are to retain our sense of what human life is. What I mean is that retention of this sense requires a quite different sort of response from that which seeks an explanation. But I shall not pursue that difficult point further here.

As for 'The Voyage to the Houyhnhnms' I am thinking especially of Gulliver's relation to the Yahoos. He was, very naturally, anxious to distance himself from these repulsive, and disconcertingly humanoid, creatures. There is a telling incident, late in his stay in the country, in which he is pursued with lustful intent by a female Yahoo while he is swimming naked in the river. At that point, he says, he could no longer conceal from himself that he was one of them. His hysterically horrified flight registers the conflict between the *necessity* and the *impossibility* of acknowledging his own common humanity with one of these depraved creatures.

The counterpart to this is the difficulty *we*, Swift's readers, have (I do not believe I am idiosyncratic in feeling this) in taking seriously — except as an intellectual *jeu d'esprit* — the completely rational Houyhnhnms. I hope I shall not be accused of "specism" if I say that we cannot relate to *horses* in the way we would have to relate to them in order to be able to recognize such qualities in them. The reason I say this is not so-called "specism" is that it has nothing whatever to do with regarding human beings as *superior* to horses. It could just as well signal the opposite of this.

We should remember that the upshot of the combined influence of Yahoos and Houyhnhnms on Gulliver was years of madness after he left their country. I think Swift knew what he was doing when he ended the story like that.

In all these cases, the situation is not that I first recognize my common humanity with others and that this recognition then provides the intellectual justification for my response to certain modalities in my dealings with them. On the contrary it is a recognition which is itself a function of those responses. In this respect it is something like Miss Anscombe's *logos* to a stopping modal. It is the point Wittgenstein is succinctly making in his remark: "My attitude towards him is an attitude towards a soul. I am not of the *opinion* that he has a soul."[7]

I want now to try to draw the threads together and see what conclusion they point to. I will express this conclusion by saying that the practical modalities to which we respond in our dealings with each other — responses which may of course be modified, blunted or intensified in particular circumstances — are akin to what Wittgenstein called "rules of grammar": perhaps even a special case of these. He spoke of the "arbitrariness" of such rules:

> Why don't I call cookery rules arbitrary, and why am I tempted to call the rules of grammar arbitrary? Because "cookery" is defined by its end, whereas "speaking" is not. That is why the use of language is in a certain sense autonomous, as cooking and washing are not. You cook badly if you are guided in your cooking by rules other than the right ones; but if you follow other rules than those of chess you are *playing another game*; and if you follow grammatical rules other than such and such ones, that does not mean that you say something wrong, no, you are speaking of something else.[8]

Analogously, we might say, the priest and the Levite saw something different from what the Samaritan saw when they came upon the injured man in the roadway. We might say: they did not see a neighbour in him. Perhaps it would sound odd to say that they did not recognize him as a fellow human being. Of course, in many contexts we would not say this. But in some contexts we do speak like this. Consider the attitudes of Europeans and white Americans to slaves in the seventeenth and eighteenth centuries. It was sometimes said of them — indeed, they sometimes said of themselves — that they did not regard slaves as human.[9] To say that is not to make a point about their competence at biological classification, though no doubt such matters were confusedly mixed up with what was really at issue, namely the nature of their moral sensibility. My central point is that in questions concerning our understanding of each other our *moral* sensibility is indeed an aspect of our *sensibility,* of the way we see things, of what we make of the world we are living in.

---

[7] *Philosophical Investigations,* Part II, Sec. iv.

[8] *Zettel* (Oxford: Basil Blackwell, 1967), para. 320.

[9] See Stanley Cavell, *The Claim of Reason* (Oxford: Oxford University Press, 1979), pp. 372–83, for an interesting discussion of this.

MORAL CONFLICT AND
POLITICAL LEGITIMACY

THOMAS NAGEL

I

Robert Frost defined a liberal as someone who can't take his own side in an argument. Though that seems a bit harsh, there is something paradoxical about liberalism, at least on the surface, and something obscure about the foundations of the sort of impartiality that liberalism professes. That is what I want to discuss.

Ethics always has to deal with the conflict between the personal standpoint of the individual and some requirement of impartiality. The personal standpoint will bring in motives derived not only from the individual's own interests but also from his personal attachments and commitments to people, projects, and particular things. The requirement of impartiality can take various forms, but it usually involves treating or counting everyone equally in some respect — according them all the same rights, or counting their good or their welfare or some aspect of it the same in determining what would be a desirable result or a permissible course of action. Since personal motives and impartiality can conflict, an ethical theory has to say something about how such conflicts are to be resolved. It may do this by according total victory to the impartial side in case of conflict, but that is only one solution.

The clash between impartiality and the viewpoint of the individual is compounded when we move from personal ethics to political theory. The reason is that in politics, where we are all competing to get the coercive power of the state behind the institutions we favour — institutions under which all of us will have to live — it is not only our personal interests, attachments, and commitments that bring us into conflict, but our different moral conceptions. Political competitors differ as to both the form and the content of the impartial component of morality. They differ over what is good and bad in human life, and what kind of equal respect or consideration we owe each other. Their political disagreements therefore reflect not only conflicts of interest but conflicts over the values that public institutions should serve, impartially, for everyone.

Is there a higher-order impartiality that can permit us to come to some understanding about how such disagreements should be settled? Or have we already gone as far as necessary (and perhaps even as far as possible) in taking up other people's point of view when we have accepted the impartial component of our own moral position? I believe that liberalism depends on the acceptance of a higher-order impartiality, and that this raises serious problems about how the different orders of impartiality are to be integrated. To some extent this parallels the familiar problem in moral theory of integrating impartiality with personal motives; but the problem here is more complicated, and the motive for higher-order impartiality is more obscure.

It is so obscure that critics of liberalism often doubt that its professions of impartiality are made in good faith. Part of the problem is that liberals ask of everyone a certain restraint in calling for the use of state power to further specific, controversial moral or religious conceptions — but the results of that restraint appear with suspicious frequency to favour precisely the controversial moral conceptions that liberals usually hold.

For example, those who argue against the restriction of pornography, or homosexuality, or contraception, or abortion on the ground that the state should not attempt to enforce contested personal standards of morality often don't think there is anything wrong with pornography, homosexuality, contraception, or abortion. They would be against such restrictions even if they believed it *was* the state's business to enforce personal morality, or if they believed that the state could legitimately be asked to prohibit anything simply on the ground that it was wrong.

More generally, liberals tend to place a high value on individual freedom, and limitations on state interference based on a higher-order impartiality among values tend to promote the individual freedom to which liberals are partial. This leads to the suspicion that the escalation to a higher level of impartiality is a sham, and that all the pleas for toleration and restraint really disguise a campaign to put the state behind a secular, individualistic, and libertine morality —

roughly speaking, against religion and in favour of sex.

Yet liberalism purports to be a view that justifies religious toleration not only to religious skeptics but to the devout, and sexual toleration not only to libertines but to those who believe extramarital sex is sinful. Its good faith is to some degree attested in the area of free expression, for there liberals in the U.S. have long defended the rights of those they detest. The A.C.L.U. is rightly glad of the chance to defend the Nazis when they want to demonstrate somewhere. It shows that liberals are willing to restrain the state from stopping something that they think is wrong — for we can assume most supporters of the A.C.L.U. think both that it's wrong to be a Nazi and that it's wrong for the Nazis to demonstrate in Skokie.

Of course liberalism is not merely a doctrine of toleration, and liberals all have more specific interests and values, some of which they will seek to support through the agency of the state. But the question of what kind of impartiality is appropriate arises there as well. Both in the prohibition of what is wrong and in the promotion of what is good, the point of view from which state action and its institutional framework are supposed to be justified is complex and in some respects obscure. I shall concentrate on the issue of toleration, and will often use the example of religious toleration. But the problem also arises in the context of distributive justice and promotion of the general welfare — for we have to use some conception of what is good for people in deciding what to distribute and what to promote.

II

Before addressing the question directly, I want to relate it to the wider issue of political legitimacy — the history of attempts over the past few centuries to discover a way of justifying coercively imposed political and social institutions to the people who have to live under them, and at the same time to discover what those institutions must be like if such justification is to be possible. These attempts have a practical motivation, since political stability is helped by wide agreement to the principles underlying a political order. But that is not all: for some, the possibility of justifying the system to as many participants as possible is of independent moral importance.

Defences of political legitimacy are of two kinds: those which discover a possible *convergence* of rational support for certain institutions from the separate motivational standpoints of distinct individuals; and those which seek a *common standpoint* that anyone can occupy, which guarantees agreement on what is acceptable. There are also political arguments that mix the convergence and common standpoint methods.

Hobbes, the founder of modern political theory, is a convergence theorist *par excellence*. Starting from a pre-moral motive that each individual has, the concern for his own survival and security, Hobbes argues that it is rational for all of us to converge from this starting point on the desirability of a system in which general obedience to certain rules of conduct is enforced by a sovereign of unlimited power. This is a convergence theory because the motive from which each of us begins refers only to his own survival and security, and it is entirely contingent that there should be any outcome that all of us can accept equally on those grounds: our personal motives could in principle fail to point us toward a common goal. And as is generally true of convergence theories, the political result is thought to be right because it is rationally acceptable to all, rather than being rationally acceptable to all because it is by some independent standard right.

Utilitarianism, on the other hand, is an example of a common standpoint theory. It asks each person to evaluate political institutions on the basis of a common moral motive which makes no reference to himself. If everyone does take up this point of view of impartial benevolence, then it will automatically follow that they all have reason to accept the same solutions — since they are evaluating them from the same point of view. A political result is then rationally acceptable to everyone because by the utilitarian standard it is right; it is not right because it is universally acceptable.

I believe that the political theories of Locke and Hume both, in their ways, mix the two methods of convergence and common standpoint. But my interest in the mixed case has to do with its importance for contemporary liberalism. Recent political philosophy has seen the development of a new type of liberal theory, exemplified by Rawls and others, whose distinctive feature is that it bases the legitimacy of institutions on their conformity to principles which it would be reasonable for disparate individuals to agree on, where the standard of individual reasonableness is not merely a pre-moral rationality, but rather a form of reasoning that includes moral motives.[1] At the same time, the moral motives which contribute to convergence are not sufficient by themselves to pick out an acceptable result: more individual motives also enter into the process. So the principles converged on are right because they are acceptable — not generally acceptable because they are by independent standards morally right.

This may seem a surprising characterization of Rawls's theory. In asking us all to enter the Original Position to choose principles of justice, he may seem to be proposing a common standpoint of impartiality which guarantees that we will all approve of the same thing. But an important element of Rawls's argument is his reference to the strains of commitment: even in the Original Position, not knowing his own conception of the good, each person can choose only such principles of justice as he believes he will be able to live under and continue to affirm in actual life, when he knows the things about himself and his position in society that are concealed by the Veil of Ignorance. True principles of justice are those which can be affirmed by individuals motivated both by the impartial sense of justice and by their fundamental personal interests, commitments, and conceptions of the good. As with other convergence theories, it is not logically guaranteed that there are such principles, but if there are, they will be shaped by the requirement of such convergence, and their rightness will not be demonstrable independently of that possibility.

I also want to take up a proposal of Scanlon's, applying to political theory what he says about contractualism as a general ethical theory in 'Contractualism and Utilitarianism'.[2] The reference to reasonable convergence occurs in his definition of moral wrongness:

> An act is wrong if its performance under the circumstances would be disallowed by any system of rules for the general regulation of behaviour which no one could reasonably reject as a basis for informed, unforced general agreement (p. 110).

"Any" here presumably means "every" rather than "some". The triple negative ("disallowed", "no one", "reject") makes the formula

---

[1] As should be obvious, I am referring here not to the reasoning inside the Original Position, but to the wider argument within which the Original Position plays a subsidiary role, the argument that we should regulate our claims on our common institutions by the principles that *would* be chosen in the Original Position.

[2] In A. Sen and B. Williams, eds., *Utilitarianism and Beyond* (Cambridge: Cambridge University Press, 1982).

rather hard to scan. But what I want to take from it is the idea of reasonable and unreasonable rejectability as a basis for assessment of rules or institutions. Notice that Scanlon doesn't say "could *rightly* reject". That would make the criterion circular. But it isn't "could *rationally* reject" either. Moral reasoning is supposed to enter into the determination of reasonableness.

An analogous standard of legitimacy would say that an illegitimate political or social institution is one that violates every principle for social assessment that no one could reasonably reject. However I'm going to dispense with some of the complications and introduce a simplified notion of legitimacy: that a political or social institution is legitimate if no one could reasonably reject it as an application of state power.

This will justify coercion of those who do not actually accept it — but only on the ground that their rejection is *unreasonable,* not just on the ground that they are *wrong* (supposing we might be convinced that they were wrong but not unreasonable). And the judgment of unreasonableness will refer not just to a common standpoint from which everyone is expected to affirm the same conclusions, but to the individual starting points of the parties, modified somewhat by common moral considerations. (In Scanlon's theory, the desire for reasonable agreement is important among those considerations.)

III

What I want to know is whether a position of this type can be made coherent and defended. I am concerned less with the specific views of Rawls or Scanlon than with the fundamental moral idea behind such a position, which is that we shouldn't impose arrangements, institutions, or requirements on other people on grounds that they could reasonably reject. This has an obvious connection with our original question concerning the sort of impartiality that liberalism requires. It is not clear why the possibility of this kind of convergence should be the standard of political legitimacy at all.

To put it simply: Why should I care whether others with whom I disagree can accept or reject the grounds on which state power is exercised? What if they hold religious or moral or cultural values that I believe to be mistaken, even though I may not be willing to claim that they are unreasonable to hold those values? Why should I allow my views of the legitimate use of state power to become hostage to what it would be reasonable for *them* to accept or reject? Why can't I instead base those views on the values that I believe to be correct?

An anti-liberal critic of Rawls could put the point by asking why he should agree to be governed by principles that he would choose if he didn't know his own religious beliefs, or his conception of the good. Isn't that being *too* impartial, giving too much authority to those whose values conflict with yours — betraying your own values, in fact? If I believe something, I believe it to be *true,* yet here I am asked to refrain from acting on that belief in deference to beliefs I think are false. What possible moral motivation could I have for doing that? Why isn't true justice giving everyone the best possible chance of salvation, for example, or a good life? In other words, don't we have to start from the values that we ourselves accept in deciding how state power may legitimately be used?

And it might be added, aren't we doing that anyway, if we adopt the liberal standard of impartiality? Not everyone believes that political legitimacy depends on this condition, and if we impose political institutions on others in our society because they do meet it (and block the imposition of institutions which do not), why aren't we being just as partial to our own values as someone who imposes a state religion?

To answer these questions we have to identify the moral conception involved and see whether it has the authority to override those more particular moral conceptions that divide us — and if so, to what extent or in what respects. Rawls has said in a recent article[3] that if liberalism had to depend on a commitment to comprehensive moral ideals of autonomy and individuality, it would become just "another sectarian doctrine" (p. 246). The question is whether its claim to be something else has any foundation.

IV

If liberalism is to be defended as a higher-order theory rather than merely as another sectarian doctrine, it must be shown to result from an interpretation of impartiality itself, rather than from a particular

---

[3] J. Rawls, 'Justice as Fairness: Political not Metaphysical', *Philosophy & Public Affairs* 14 (1985).

conception of the good that is to be made impartially available. Of
course any interpretation of impartiality will be morally controversial
— it is not a question of rising to a vantage point above all moral
disputes — but the controversy will be at a different level.

What form should impartiality take, in the special conditions which
are the province of political theory? The specialness of the conditions
is important. We have to be impartial not just in the conferring of
benefits, but in the imposition of burdens, the exercise of coercion to
insure compliance with a uniform set of requirements, and the demand
for support of the institutions that impose those requirements and
exercise that coercion. (Even if the support is not voluntarily given,
it will to some degree be exacted, if only through payment of taxes
and passive conformity to certain institutional arrangements.)

If someone wishes simply to benefit others, there can in my view be
no objection if he gives them what is good by his own lights (so long
as he does them no harm by theirs). If someone wants to pray for the
salvation of my soul, I can't really complain on the ground that I would
rather he gave me a subscription to *Hustler*. The problem arises when
he wants to force me to attend church or pay for its upkeep instead of
staying home and reading *Hustler*. The real problem is how to justify
making people do things against their will.

We can leave aside the familiar and unproblematic Hobbesian basis
for coercion: I may want to be forced to do something as part of a
practice whereby everyone else is forced to do the same, with results
that benefit us all in a way that would not be possible unless we could
be assured of widespread compliance. This is not really forcing people
to do what they don't want to do, but rather enabling them to do
what they want to do by forcing them to do it.

There are two other types of coercion whose justification seems
clear: prevention of harm to others and certain very basic forms of
paternalism. In both these types of case, we can make an impersonal
appeal to values that are generally shared: people don't want to be
injured, robbed, or killed, and they don't want to get sick. The impersonal value of avoiding those harms is uncontroversial, and can be
appealed to in order to justify forcibly preventing their infliction. From
an impersonal standpoint I can agree that anyone, myself included,
should be prevented from harming others in those ways.

I can also agree that under some conditions I should be prevented from harming myself in those ways, as should anyone else. The clear conditions include my being crazy or demented in some fairly drastic degree, or radically misinformed about the likely results of what I am doing. Paternalism is justified in such cases because when we look at them from outside, we find no impersonal value competing with the values of health, life, and safety. If I say I would want to be prevented from drinking lye during a psychotic episode, it is not because the dangers of internal corrosion outweigh the value of self-expression. We are not faced here with a conflict of impartialities.

But in other cases we are. I've gone over these familiar examples for the sake of contrast. There are cases where forcing someone to do what he doesn't want to do is problematic — not just because he doesn't want to do it, but because of his reasons for not wanting to do it.[4] The problematic cases are those in which either the impersonal value to which I appeal to justify coercion would not be acknowledged by the coercee, or else it conflicts with another impersonal value to which he subscribes but which I do not acknowledge, though I would if I were he. In such a case it seems that I will have failed in some respect to be impartial whether I coerce him or not.

An example may help. I am not a Christian Scientist. If I ask myself whether, thinking of it from outside, I would want to be forced to undergo medical treatment if I *were* a Christian Scientist and had a treatable illness, it's hard to know what to say. On the one hand, given my beliefs, I am inclined to give no impersonal weight to the reasons I would offer for refusing treatment if I were a Christian Scientist, and substantial weight to the medical reasons in favour of treatment. After all, if I believe Christian Science is false, I believe it would be false even if I believed it was true. On the other hand, I am inclined to give considerable impersonal weight to the broader consideration of not wanting others to ride roughshod over my beliefs on the subject of religion, whatever they may be.

Or suppose a Roman Catholic, who believes that outside the Church there is no salvation, asks himself whether if he were not a Catholic he would want to be given strong incentives to accept the Catholic faith,

---

[4] Other people's preferences *per se* don't always provide us with an impersonal reason to consider them. Here I agree with Scanlon against Hare and others. See T. M. Scanlon, 'Preference and Urgency', *Journal of Philosophy* 72 (1975), and R. M. Hare, *Moral Thinking* (Oxford: Oxford University Press, 1981), Chap. 5.

perhaps by state support of the Church and legal discouragement of other religions.[5] He may be torn between the impartial application of his actual religious values, and the impartial application of a more general value that he also holds, of not wanting other people's religious convictions to be imposed on him.

Which of these should dominate? It is really a problem about the interpretation of the familiar role reversal argument in ethics: "How would you like it if someone did that to you?" The answer that has to be dealt with is, "How would I like it if someone did *what* to me?" There is often more than one way of describing a proposed course of action, and much depends on which description is regarded as relevant for the purpose of moral argument.

V

This general problem is familiar in the context of interpreting universalizability conditions in ethics, but I am thinking of a particular version of it. Should a Catholic, considering restriction of freedom of worship and religious education for Protestants from an impersonal standpoint, think of what he is doing as

(1) preventing them from putting themselves and others in danger of eternal damnation
(2) promoting adherence to the true faith
(3) promoting adherence to the Catholic faith
(4) preventing them from practising their religion
(5) preventing them from doing something they want to do?

As far as he is concerned, he is doing all of these things. Which of them determines how he should judge his action from an impersonal standpoint?

The defence of liberalism depends on rejecting (5) as the relevant description, and then stopping with (4) rather than going on to (2) or (1). Roughly, the liberal position avoids two contrary errors. To accept as an authoritative impersonal value everyone's interest in

---

[5] "He would want", in these examples, is not a conditional prediction of what his desires would be in those circumstances: rather, it refers to what he *now* wants to happen in those counterfactual circumstances — as in the statement, "I would want to be restrained if I tried to drink lye during a psychotic episode." The "want" goes outside rather than inside the conditional.

doing what he wants to do, for whatever reason, (i.e. (5)), is to give too much authority to individual preferences in determining other people's claims on us. To accord impersonal weight to our own values, whatever they are (i.e. (1) and (2)), is on the other hand not to give others enough authority over their claims on us for restraint.

The characteristic of description (4) that the others lack is that it has some chance of both (a) being accepted by all parties concerned as a true description of what is going on (something it shares with (3) and (5)), and (b) being accorded the same kind of impersonal value by all parties concerned (something it shares, more or less, with (1) and (2)).

This makes (4) a natural choice for the morally relevant description which provides a basis for impartial assessment. However there are several objections that have to be dealt with.

First, why isn't (5) at least as impartial as (4)? No one wants to be prevented from doing what he wants to do. Why can't we all agree that impersonal value should be assigned to people doing or getting what they want, rather than to something more restricted like freedom of worship?

But the fact is that we can't. To assign impersonal value to the satisfaction of all preferences is to accept a particular view of the good — a component of one form of utilitarianism — which many would find clearly unacceptable and which they would not be unreasonable to reject. The objection to making it the basis of political legitimacy parallels the objection to making any other comprehensive individual conception of the good the basis of political and social institutions. A liberal who is a utilitarian should no more impose his conception of the good on others than should a liberal who is a Roman Catholic or a devotee of aesthetic perfection — that is, he should pursue the good so conceived for himself and others only within the limits imposed by a higher order impartiality.

This reply, however, leads to another objection: If (5) is ruled out, why shouldn't (4) be ruled out for parallel reasons? The problem with assigning impersonal value to the satisfaction of preferences *per se* (i.e. (5)) is that if a non-utilitarian is asked, "How would you like to be prevented from doing something you want to do?" he can reply, "That depends on what it is, and why I want to do it." A similar move might be made against assigning uniform impersonal value to religious toleration (i.e. (4)). If a Catholic is asked, "How would you like to be prevented from practicing your religion?" why can't he reply, "That depends on whether it's the true religion or not"?

But in that case we are left with no version of what is going on that permits a common description resulting in a common impersonal assessment. If the description can be agreed on the assessment can't be, and *vice versa.* Impartiality has been ruled out.

VI

The defence of liberalism requires that a limit somehow be drawn to appeals to *the truth* in political argument. It may seem paradoxical that a general condition of impartiality should claim greater authority than more special conceptions which one believes to be, simply, true — and that it should lead us to defer to conceptions which we believe to be false — but that is the position.

This issue is discussed in Gerald Dworkin's essay, 'Non-neutral Principles'.[6] He has in mind principles like "The true religion should be taught in the public schools" — whose "application to particular cases is a matter of controversy for the parties whose conduct is supposed to be regulated by the principle in question."[7]

Dworkin argues that the liberal position has to rest on an epistemological premise: "that one cannot arrive at justified belief in religious matters."[8] That, he claims, is the only possible justification for suppressing knowledge of the parties' religious beliefs in Rawls's Original Position — a condition which is essential to Rawls's argument for tolerance. "If there were a truth and it could be ascertained," he asks, "would those in the original position who contemplated the possibility that they would be holders of false views regard their integrity as harmed by choosing that it should be suppressed?"[9]

Rawls, however, claims that his position depends on no such skepticism.[10] "We may observe," he adds, "that men's having an equal liberty of conscience is consistent with the idea that all men ought

---

[6] G. Dworkin, 'Non-neutral Principles', *Journal of Philosophy* 71 (1974).

[7] Op. cit., p. 492.

[8] Ibid., p. 505.

[9] Ibid., p. 503–4.

[10] *A Theory of Justice* (Cambridge, Mass.: Harvard University Press, 1972), pp. 214–15.

to obey God and accept the truth. The problem of liberty is that of choosing a principle by which the claims men make on one another in the name of their religion are to be regulated. Granting that God's will should be followed and the truth recognized does not as yet define a principle of adjudication."[11]

He intends to put forward not a skeptical position about religious knowledge but a restriction on the sorts of convictions that can be appealed to in political argument. In the 1985 paper he says, "It is important to stress that from other points of view, for example, from the point of view of personal morality, or from the point of view of members of an association, or of one's religious or philosophical doctrine, various aspects of the world and one's relation to it, may be regarded in a different way. But these other points of view are not to be introduced into political discussion."[12]

I believe that true liberalism requires that something like Rawls's view be correct, i.e that exclusion of the appeal to religious convictions not rely on a skeptical premise. As I have said, liberalism should provide the devout with a reason for tolerance. But is Rawls right? It isn't enough to exclude knowledge of one's religious beliefs from the Original Position on the ground that this is needed to make agreement possible. The question is whether there is a viable form of impartiality that makes it possible to exclude such factors from the basis of one's acceptance of political institutions, or whether, alternatively, we have to give up the hope of liberal legitimacy.

I believe that the demand for agreement, and its priority in these cases over a direct appeal to the truth, must be grounded in something more basic. Though it has to do with epistemology, it is not skepticism. Rather it might be thought of as a matter of epistemological restraint: the distinction between what an individual can be justified in believing (i.e. holding to be true), and what he can legitimately use as a premise in justification of what he does to others against their will.

A distinction of this kind results, I believe, if we combine the general picture of moral thought that underlies liberalism with the familiar fact that while I cannot ascribe a belief to myself without implying that what I believe is true, there is a big difference, looking at it from the outside, between my believing something and its being true.

---

[11] Op. cit., p. 217–8.
[12] 'Justice as Fairness: Political not Metaphysical' (op. cit.), p. 231.

On the view I would defend, there is a highest-order framework of moral reasoning which takes us outside ourselves to a standpoint that is independent of who we are. It cannot derive its basic premises from aspects of our particular and contingent starting points within the world, though it may authorize reliance on such specialized points of view from the more universal perspective. Since individuals are very different from one another and must lead complex individual lives, the universal standpoint cannot reasonably withhold this authorization lightly. But it is most likely to be withheld from attempts to claim the authority of the impersonal standpoint for a point of view that is in fact that of a particular individual or party, against that of other individuals or parties who reject it. This happens especially in the political or social imposition of institutions that control our lives, that we cannot escape, and that are maintained by force.

Morality can take us outside of ourselves in different ways or to different degrees. The first and most familiar step is to recognize that what we want should not depend only on our own interests and desires — that from outside other people's interests matter as much as yours do, and you should want to reconcile your interests with theirs as far as possible. But liberal impartiality goes beyond this, by trying to make the epistemological standpoint of morality impersonal as well.

The idea is that when we look at certain of our convictions from outside, the appeal to their truth must be seen merely as an appeal to our beliefs, and should be treated as such unless they can be shown to be justifiable from a more impersonal standpoint. If not, they have to remain, for the purpose of a certain kind of moral argument, features of a personal perspective — to be respected as such but no more than that.

This doesn't mean we have to stop believing them — i.e. believing them to be *true*. Considered as individual beliefs they may be adequately grounded, or at least not unreasonable; the standards of epistemological ethics are different from the standards of epistemology itself. It means only that from the perspective of political argument we may have to regard certain of our beliefs, whether moral or religious or even historical or scientific, as simply someone's beliefs, rather than as truths — unless they can be given the kind of impersonal justification appropriate to that perspective, in which case they may be appealed to as truths without qualification.[13]

Thus in certain contexts I am constrained to make use of the distinction between my believing something and its being true, and to consider my beliefs merely as beliefs rather than as truths, however convinced I may be that they are true, and that I know it. This is not to adopt a general skepticism about my beliefs. Of course if I believe something I believe it to be true. I can recognize the possibility that what I believe may be false, but I can't with respect to any particular present belief of mine think that possibility is realized. Nevertheless, for certain purposes I can distinguish my attitude toward my belief from my attitude toward the thing believed, and can refer only to my belief rather than to its truth in certain contexts of argument.

The reason is that unless there is some way of applying from an impersonal standpoint the distinction between my believing something and its being true, an appeal to its truth is equivalent to an appeal to my belief in its truth. To show that this was not so I would have to show how the distinction could be applied, in political argument, in a way that did not surreptitiously assume my personal starting point — by for example defining objective truth in terms of the religion to which I adhere, or the beliefs I now hold. I have to be able to admit that I might turn out to be wrong, by some standards that those who disagree with me but are also committed to the impersonal standpoint can also acknowledge. The appeal to truth as opposed to belief is compatible with disagreement among the parties — but it must imply the possibility of some standard which could in principle be impersonally applied, even if it cannot settle our disagreement at the moment.

Admittedly it will be controversial in many cases whether an appeal to truth collapses into an appeal to belief — some people might try to deny objective status to scientific methods that most of us would take as clear cases of impersonal verification, whereas others might claim objective status for certain theological arguments or forms of revelation. These issues have to be argued out one by one; I do not have a general account of an impersonal epistemological standard. But

---

[13] I don't know whether I'm prepared to claim that the standard of liberal impartiality itself meets this condition of impersonal justifiability. This much can be said, however: its claim to impersonal validity is not undermined by the fact that some people may not accept it because they reject the requirement of impersonal justifiability itself.

the basic idea remains intelligible even if its application is problematic. The appeal to truth in political argument requires an objective distinction between belief and truth that can be applied from the impersonal standpoint appropriate to the argument in question.

Otherwise it becomes an appeal to what I believe, and belief carries a very different kind of weight in such arguments. The fact that someone has certain religious or moral convictions has its own considerable importance, from an impersonal standpoint, in determining how he should be treated and what he should do, but it is not the same as the importance that the truth of those convictions would have, if it could be admitted as a premise in political argument. There would be no inclination to accept impersonally a general right to try to use state power to limit the liberty of others to force them to live as I *believe* they should live. None of us would be willing to have our liberty limited by others on such grounds. But if I am right, the appeal to the truth of a certain religion to justify enforcement collapses into just such an appeal to belief.

VII

Even if some form of liberal impartiality can be defended in this way, it has to contend with the persistence of those personal convictions which it excludes from political argument, or admits only under strict constraints. This is a general problem in ethics: the impersonal standpoint doesn't make personal motives go away, and in restricting their operation it may put itself under great strain.

It is difficult to decide how much weight the liberal version of impartiality can bear when it comes into conflict not only with purely personal interests but with the impartial application of more particular values that cannot be generally acknowledged. From an impersonal standpoint, how strongly is my commitment to religious toleration prepared to resist the value of health, when applied to the case of a Christian Scientist? And how strongly can the impersonal value of not being prevented from practising one's religion resist the less impartial but still impersonal interest of a Catholic in the salvation of souls? Or to take a current example, can a politically liberal Catholic subordinate his conviction that abortion is grievously wrong to the principle that sectarian moral positions should not be appealed to to justify limits on the liberty of those who reject them?

This example illustrates the great difficulty of applying liberal principles. That outlawing abortion is a significant limitation of liberty which requires justification is not controversial. That there is such a justification — i.e. that abortion is a prohibited taking of innocent human life — is highly controversial, and it is not at all clear whether it admits of an impersonal distinction between belief and truth, even though many of the arguments are not religious. However if one has the belief, the wrongness of abortion is likely to seem much more important than the value of individual liberty, however impersonally acceptable the latter may be by comparison.

Liberalism is a demanding doctrine. Still, it is qualified somewhat by a division of the moral territory. Its relatively stringent impartiality applies only to uniform and involuntary social and political institutions. One might ask why. Why doesn't the same standard apply to the justification of all action that has an effect, even indirect, on the interests of others? I have only the vague answer that this is another instance of the moral division of labour between society and the individual, corresponding to the division of standpoints in each of us.[14]

We literally externalize the demands of the impersonal standpoint by placing in the hands of social and political institutions the task of enforcing the most general claims for assistance and restraint of our fellow human beings. Subject to our contribution to the support of those institutions, this ideally should leave us free to lead our individual lives in obedience to more personal attachments, commitments, and crotchets. It would be for most of us intolerably intrusive to have to live by a morality that required us to justify everything we did, insofar as it affected others, in terms that could be defended from an impersonal standpoint.

The liberal restriction on what kind of thing we may appeal to does not apply to the justification of action generally. It leaves individuals free to regulate their own personal lives (and to a lesser extent, though this is a problematic intermediate case, the lives of their children) according to their full personal conceptions of how life should be lived. And it also, importantly, leaves them free to refer to their own conceptions in determining how they will benefit others or help

---

[14] See T. Nagel, *The View From Nowhere* (Oxford: Oxford University Press, 1986), pp. 188, 206–7.

them avoid harm or misfortune, so far as this goes beyond what is morally or legally obligatory.

Most importantly of all, this extends to the domain of political activity which is left open in a democracy to the pursuit by individuals of their goals and interests — the large range of legislative and communal issues that are put under the control of the preferences of the majority, or of coalitions among minorities. In these cases it is not that we give the authority of the impersonal standpoint to the point of view of the winning side. Rather, on a certain range of questions, we regard the balancing of all sorts of personal preferences or opinions against one another as impersonally acceptable.

Liberalism certainly does not require us to run our lives, even our lives as political beings, on radically impartial principles. But it does require that the framework within which we pursue our more individual values and subject ourselves to the possibility of control by the values of others be in a strong sense impartially justifiable. That means it must bear up under substantial moral and motivational strain.

The real issue is not just relative strength but relative priority. Liberal impartiality is not in competition with more specific values as one conception of the good among others. If it were, it would be unintelligible, for it would have to advocate impartiality between itself and alternative conceptions, and this would generate a meaningless regress of higher-order standpoints in search of common ground between liberalism and more sectarian views. But liberalism does not require its adherents to step outside liberalism itself to compromise with anti-liberal positions. It purports to provide a maximally impartial standard of right which has priority over more specialized conceptions in determining what may be imposed on us by our fellow humans, and *vice versa*.[15]

Of course liberal impartiality claims for itself an authority that will not in fact be universally accepted, and therefore the justifications it offers for resisting the imposition of more particular values in certain cases will not secure actual universal agreement. But since it is a substantive moral position, that is not surprising.

---

[15] This is not just the familiar doctrine of priority of the right over the good, since some of the specialized views that are subordinated by liberalism may themselves be conceptions of right.

INTERSUBJECTIVITY AND REASON

ALBRECHT WELLMER

I

In § 40 of his *Critique of Judgment,* entitled 'On Taste as a Kind of *Sensus Communis*', Kant formulates three "maxims" of what he calls "common human understanding"; they are: "1. To think for oneself; 2. To think from the standpoint of everybody else; 3. Always to think in agreement with oneself."[1] These three maxims, concerning (1) the autonomy, (2) the intersubjective validity, and (3) the coherence of our thinking, could, I think, be understood as expressing Kant's *normative* conception of reason. By a normative conception of reason I do not just mean practical reason in the Kantian sense, but a conception of those demands under which beings find themselves who have the *faculty* of reason, i.e. rational beings in the Kantian sense. The three maxims are maxims concerning the right *use* of the faculty of reason in any possible domain of its application. They express the most general standards of rational thought and, because of the internal link between thinking and acting, of rational behaviour in general; standards which human beings often fall short of and which correspondingly define a practical *task* implied in the faculty of reason. Since Kant's maxims concern the *use* we make of the faculty of reason they could also be called maxims of practical reason, the term "practical reason" here taken in its broadest possible sense.

As to its normative content the maxim of autonomous thinking is, I believe, at once the most obvious and the most difficult one to explain. But I shall not discuss it here. I simply take it for granted that it is a legitimate expression of a fundamental Enlightenment concern with the potential autonomy of all rational beings. However, I want to say a few words about the second and the third maxim. The third maxim is not just a restatement of the law of non-contradiction, it could rather

---

[1] Immanuel Kant, *The Critique of Judgment,* trans. by J. C. Meredith (Oxford: Clarendon Press, 1952), p. 152.

be understood as a "projection" of this law onto the three-dimensional space of the life of individuals, who, as rational beings, at any point of time can be characterized by a totality of beliefs, attitudes and goals of action, and who furthermore cannot help but relate to their own past and future, ultimately to their own life as a whole. The maxim of coherence is not so much concerned with the problem of illogical thinking as it demands that I confront my various beliefs, attitudes, goals and actions which, if they are contradictory among each other, cannot be legitimate beliefs, attitudes, goals and actions all at the same time. Of course, it does not say that I must not change *my* beliefs, attitudes or ways of acting over time, but it demands that I recognize my past beliefs, etc. as my beliefs, etc., so that I am always confronted with the problem of how I got from "there" to "here" and therefore with the problem of the coherence of my life over time. I must confess that I used to be puzzled about Kant's statement, which he makes shortly after formulating the three maxims of common human understanding, that the third maxim is the hardest to live up to. But the more I think about it the more I think that Kant might have been right, for this maxim, if I am not mistaken, concerns the problem of rationality with respect to what today is often called the problem of personal identity, i.e., the problem of how we can affirmatively relate to our life as a whole.

I have briefly talked about Kant's third maxim to establish a kind of very sketchy frame of reference for what follows. Basically, however, I want to talk about the second maxim, which Kant also calls the maxim of an "enlarged way of thinking", or of an "enlarged mind", as it is usually rendered in the English translation. It is the maxim of "reflective judgment", the function of which is to ensure the intersubjective validity of our thoughts, to keep it within the bounds of the "*sensus communis*". "By the name *sensus communis*," Kant explains,

is to be understood the idea of a *public* sense, i.e., a critical faculty which in its reflective act takes into account (*a priori*) the mode of representation of everyone else, in order, *as it were,* to weigh its judgment with the collective reason of mankind, and thereby avoid the illusion arising from subjective and personal conditions which would readily be taken for objective, an illusion that would exert a prejudicial influence upon its judgment. This is accomplished by weighing its judgment, not so much with the actual, as rather with the merely possible, judgments of others, and by putting ourselves in the position of everyone else, as the result of a mere abstraction from the limitations which contingently affect our own estimate.[2]

Interestingly enough, although Kant lists the maxim of "reflective judgment" among his three maxims of common human understanding, reflective judgment appears in his philosophy almost exclusively in its *transcendental* functions, e.g., in his theory of aesthetic judgment. The reason for this, I think, is what I would call Kant's transcendental solipsism. Kant's transcendental subject is, conceptually speaking, a subject conceived of in the singular mode. This means that for Kant the intersubjective validity of our theoretical or moral judgments is widely guaranteed by formal conditions which can either be explained without reference to an essential plurality of subjects or which, as in Kant's moral philosophy, refer to other subjects only as to other embodiments of the same noumenal Ego. But then to think from the standpoint of everyone else amounts to thinking from the standpoint of a purified subject, i.e., a subject purified from all those idiosyncratic conditions (emotions, passions, biographical and historical limitations, etc.) which pertain to subjects as empirical, that is embodied beings. The purified subject *is* the transcendental or noumenal Ego.

Now it seems to me — and I shall argue later on — that the idea of a transcendental subject of cognition, a subject conceived in the singular mode, has strong historical and conceptual affinities to the idea of a solitary speaker. By a solitary speaker I mean a speaker who is the *only* speaker of his language in the following sense: he is not, and never has been, a member of a linguistic community through which he has learned his language and through which he has acquired a conception of himself as one among other — actual or potential — speakers. To distinguish such a solitary speaker from a speaker who only happens to live in complete isolation from other human beings *with* whom he could speak — e.g. like Robinson Crusoe — one might call this solitary speaker an "essentially solitary speaker". According to one interpretation of Wittgenstein's so-called "private language argument", an interpretation which has recently been defended by Baker, Hacker, McGinn and others, this argument as well as Wittgenstein's reflections on rule-following in general leave open the conceptual possibility of such an essentially solitary speaker,

---

[2] Ibid., p. 151.

provided only that the rules of language which this solitary speaker is following could *in principle* be learned by other human beings: i.e., the rules of this language may be "private" in the sense that the solitary speaker is the only one who ever followed them, although they must not be private in the sense that nobody else could possibly understand and follow these rules. If we grant these presuppositions we might say that the solitary speaker could also in principle obey Kant's maxim of reflective judgment insofar as he could refer in his thinking to *possible* other speakers of his language. Reflection on his judgments from the standpoint of everyone else would mean for him reflection on his judgments from the standpoint of every other possible speaker of his language — and this seems in fact to be something analogous to reflecting on one's judgments from the standpoint of *the* transcendental subject.

In what follows I first want to raise some objections against this idea of an essentially solitary speaker. I shall argue that such a solitary speaker — whatever it may be that he does when he uses his "language" — could not possibly conceive of himself *as* a speaker and therefore in an important sense could not be *called* a speaker. In other words, our concepts of meaning, understanding, and truth, and therefore our concept of language, would not be applicable to him because he himself lacks the corresponding concepts, and to acquire them he would have to learn "our" language (i.e., one of our languages). Of course, we could in *some* sense relate to him as a speaker, "take him into our community", as Kripke would say, as we sometimes do with animals or computers, but this would at best be a way of *making* him a speaker, i.e., of introducing him into our language. My argument will have some affinity to an argument put forward by Davidson,[3] but I shall develop it in terms which are rather suggested by Wittgenstein and by Kripke's interpretation of Wittgenstein.[4] To put it simply, although somewhat misleadingly: I shall argue for a Davidsonian thesis by defending a Kripkean version of the private language argument. The Davidsonian thesis is, that "a creature cannot have thoughts unless it is an interpreter of the speech of another"[5]; a thesis which can

---

[3] Donald Davidson, 'Thought and Talk', in Donald Davidson, *Inquiries into Truth and Interpretation* (Oxford: Clarendon Press, 1985), pp. 155–170.

[4] Saul A. Kripke, *Wittgenstein on Rules and Private Language* (Oxford: Basil Blackwell, 1982).

[5] Davidson, op. cit., p. 157.

also be expressed by saying that the contrast between truth and error requires the context of a speech community, since it "can emerge only in the context of interpretation, which alone forces us to the idea of an objective, public truth".[6] In contrast to Davidson, however, I do not believe that meaning can be explained in terms of truth conditions. I shall therefore rather follow Wittgenstein and Kripke in stating my argument. Having criticized the idea of a solitary speaker I hope to show how this critique bears on the idea of a transcendental subject of cognition. In subsequent sections of my paper I shall first, briefly, try to point out in which respect my conceptual strategy differs from that of Davidson and then point to some implications of my argument concerning the idea of rationality. At this point I shall come back to Kant's second maxim of common human understanding and then try to give it a somewhat un-Kantian twist.

II

What I have called the Kripkean version of the private language argument has been summed up by Kripke when he says: "What is really denied [i.e., by the private language argument, A.W.] is what might be called the 'private model' of rule following, that the notion of a person following a given rule is to be analysed simply in terms of facts about the rule follower and the rule follower alone, without reference to his membership in a wider community."[7] Kripke is concerned with the question, under which conditions we may assert statements like "X means P by 'S'"; and Kripke's answer, to put it very roughly, is that the decisive condition for the assertability of such statements is that X's use of 'S' sufficiently agrees with *our* understanding of P. So we are — provisionally — entitled to say that X means addition by "plus" if X uses the sign "plus" as an addition sign in our sense, which also means that X gives a sufficient number of correct responses to addition problems, correct, in other words, according to *our* criteria of correctness. In a similar way one might say that the assertability condition for "X has grasped the concept of addition" is that X comes up with a sufficient number of correct responses to addition problems, "correct" obviously again meaning correct according to *our* criteria

---

[6] Ibid., p. 170.
[7] Kripke, op. cit., p. 109.

of correctness. Accordingly Kripke claims that in our "third person use" of words like "understanding", "meaning", etc. we do not refer to individuals in isolation, but as actual or potential members of our linguistic community, taking them into our community, as it were. This position might be characterized as a "community view" of our language game with the words "understanding" and "meaning", but by implication — and in a sense which has yet to be clarified — we may also call it a community view of language.

Now given a certain minimal agreement concerning the interpretation of what Wittgenstein says about rules, meaning and understanding — an agreement which actually exists between Kripke and his critics, — Kripke's basic claims seem to me to be almost trivially true. And yet he has been severely attacked for his interpretation of what he takes to be Wittgenstein's community view of language. To bring out the crucial point of his argument as I see it I want to briefly discuss two counterarguments which are both concerned with defending the idea of a solitary speaker. But first I want to say a few words about the minimal agreement between Kripke and his critics to which I have alluded above. This agreement concerns certain important conclusions Wittgenstein drew from the fact that, as far as the application of rules is concerned, justification must come to an end. These conclusions are stated in *Philosophical Investigations,* paras 201 and 219:

> 201. This was our paradox: no course of action could be determined by a rule, because every course of action can be made out to accord with the rule. The answer was: if everything can be made out to accord with the rule, then it can also be made out to conflict with it. And so there would be neither accord nor conflict here.
>
> It can be seen that there is a misunderstanding here from the mere fact that in the course of our argument we give one interpretation after another; as if each contented us at least for a moment, until we thought of yet another standing behind it. What this shows is that there is a way of grasping a rule which is *not* an *interpretation*, but which is exhibited in what we call 'obeying the rule' and 'going against it' in actual cases.
>
> Hence there is an inclination to say: every action according to the rule is an interpretation. But we ought to restrict the term 'interpretation' to the substitution of one expression of the rule for another.
>
> 219. ... When I obey a rule, I do not choose. I obey the rule *blindly.*

My claim that there exists an agreement between Kripke and his critics about the interpretation of these passages may sound preposterous.

But I think it must be granted as true, once we neglect some of the misunderstandings which have come up in the discussion of Kripke's book. However, I shall not argue this point. The real disagreement between Kripke and his critics, as I see it, concerns the interpretation of para. 202 and the conclusions to be drawn from it:

> 202. And hence also 'obeying a rule' is a practice. And to *think* one is obeying a rule is not to obey a rule. Hence it is not possible to obey a rule 'privately': otherwise thinking one was obeying a rule would be the same thing as obeying it.

Without further preliminaries I now want to discuss the two counterarguments against Kripke which I have mentioned above. The first counterargument draws on Wittgenstein's insight that understanding a word is akin to an ability. The argument then says that attributing an ability — e.g., the ability to use certain words according to a rule — does not involve reference to a community; furthermore, since an isolated person may very well be aware of having or not having certain abilities, a solitary speaker might very well — without any reference to a community — know what he means by certain words. As Baker and Hacker have put it:

> One's confidence in one's mastery of a technique which one displays daily rests on just that fact — that one displays it, exercises this skill, daily. And if 'W' is a word in a language which, as it happens, only Robinson Crusoe speaks, the case does not essentially differ. The question concerns one's certainty about one's possession of (the continuity of) an ability or skill. And inasmuch as one exercises the skill frequently, one is typically perfectly confident, and rightly so. There is no room here for a serious skeptical foothold.[8]

Now considering what this argument is meant to prove, it seems to me to be so obviously fallacious that I want to discuss it only very briefly. The fallacy consists in a false analogy between certain physical abilities or skills and *understanding* as an ability. Let us take the ability to swim. I may be quite confident that I (still) have the ability to swim; but having this conviction I might also find out some day that I do not really have this ability (any more). There are certain criteria for having this ability which I know if I know what "swimming"

---

[8] G. P. Baker and P. M. S. Hacker, *Skepticism, Rules and Language* (Oxford: Basil Blackwell, 1984), p. 78.

means. But what about *this* ability (I mean my knowledge of what "swimming" means)? Whether I have this ability I evidently cannot find out by going into the water. So if I am a solitary speaker *how* do I convince myself daily that I am still able to use the words of my language correctly? Here Baker and Hacker could only answer: By using them with confidence. But then, in contrast to the first case — my confidence about my ability to swim — it does not seem to be clear what would count as a *disconfirmation* of my confidence; for "whatever is going to seem right to me is right".[9] Understood as an argument against a community view of language the argument can therefore be dismissed as simply begging the question.

The second counterargument against Kripke which I want to discuss is in a way more interesting than the first one, because it will lead us directly beyond a mere restatement of the terms of the controversy. The argument basically consists of an initial, and legitimate, distinction, from which an illegitimate conclusion is derived. The legitimate distinction is one which Kenny had already emphasized in his book on Wittgenstein, namely that "'A kept the rule' and 'Everybody agreed that A kept the rule' have different meanings".[10] The illegitimate conclusion is that statements like "X means P by 'S'" do not involve reference to a community. The intermediate step, which connects the initial distinction with the conclusion, is a "performative" reformulation of the "community agreement condition" which then seems to make it redundant. As McGinn has put it:

> The claim, then, is that I will judge that you (e.g.) mean addition by 'plus' if and only if I observe that your responses with 'plus' agree with mine sufficiently often (or with those of the community to which I belong). My first objection to this is that the reference to my own responses is strictly *redundant* in this assertability condition: for the correct condition is simply that I observe that you give the *sum* of pairs of numbers sufficiently often.[11]

What McGinn is arguing is that, although it is true that if I say that "you give the sum of pairs of numbers sufficiently often", I am

---

[9] Ludwig Wittgenstein, *Philosophical Investigations*, trans. by G. E. M. Anscombe (Oxford: Basil Blackwell, 1958), para 258.

[10] Anthony Kenny, *Wittgenstein* (Cambridge, Mass.: Harvard University Press, 1973), p. 174.

[11] Colin McGinn, *Wittgenstein on Meaning* (Oxford: Basil Blackwell, 1984), p. 185.

implying that "you give the sum of pairs of numbers sufficiently often according to *my* (our) criteria of correct adding", reference to my (our) criteria of correct adding — i.e., ultimately to my own (our) responses — is redundant in the statement of assertability conditions, because my (our) criteria of correct adding are obviously the only ones I could possibly use when stating that somebody has given the sum of pairs of numbers. Now this, as far as it goes, seems to be correct; accordingly McGinn's conclusion also seems to be justified, viz., that the assertability condition (for "S means P by 'S'") is therefore "entirely individualistic in that it refers only to the person to whom the rule is ascribed and to his behaviour — no mention here of me or my community".[12] The interesting thing, however, is that, if the "anti-community thesis" is stated in this way, it implies — contrary to what McGinn assumes — the community thesis in the Kripkean (and Wittgensteinian) sense. Correctly understood, that is, the two become indistinguishable. Let me try to show this.

The decisive point which has already been granted in the argument which I have quoted is that statements about somebody's correct or incorrect rule following involve an application of the *same* rule by the person who makes the statement. I can only say that "X means P by 'S'" if I have a concept of P which I must apply to find out whether X's use of "S" amounts to his following the rules for P. Now let me take it for granted that *my* understanding of P is *our* understanding of P. It is then, of course, *our* responses which ultimately determine my judgment about whether X is following the rules for P (whether he means P by "S"). Although I do not refer to our community if I say that X uses "plus" (correctly) as an addition-sign, it is my (our) understanding of addition which determines my judgment. Contrary to what the "anti-communitarian" assumes, however, this is not a trivial matter, as can be seen if we think of certain possible variations in the conditions for concept attributions.

Let me first assume that X's language is different from mine (I am Friday meeting Robinson Crusoe), and I try to learn X's language. As time goes on I shall form certain expectations about X's use of certain words, which I might occasionally state in the form "X means P by 'S'". If now X's actual use of "S" at certain occasions deviates from my expectations, I shall, up to a point, decide, not that X uses

---

[12] Ibid.

"S" incorrectly (because not in accordance with my understanding of P), but that he does not really mean P by "S". This is the stage where I still try to learn X's language; so here X is the teacher and I am the pupil. But certainly this cannot go on forever; for learning a language means at some point that one becomes a competent speaker oneself. Once I have reached this point we have, as it were, become equals. Having learned what X means by "S", I have learned the meaning of "S" (in his language, which has become my language as well). From now on there are always *two* possibilities if X's use of language deviates from my expectations: I could *either* come to the conclusion that X did not use a word in its usual sense, i.e., in the way I understood it — and then X could explain to me *how* he used it; *or* I could come to the conclusion that X did not use the word correctly — and then I should in principle be able to convince him of *that.* The two of us now form a linguistic community where each of us may feel entitled, on certain occasions, to correct the other according to the way each of us understands our common language, or in which each of us can explain to the other how he meant a certain word on a specific occasion. Under these conditions — which are the conditions of a common language — I usually take it for granted that X means, for example, *red* by "red", *house* by "house", *love* by "love", and *plus* by "plus" — i.e., according to *my* understanding of these words, which I take for granted is *our* understanding of these words. This is not an observer's hypothesis (any more), but rather a tacit presupposition which is constitutive of our being able to talk *with each other.* It is on the basis of this presupposition that we can correct each other, disagree with each other, give explanations to each other, and also form explicit hypotheses like "X means P by 'S'" on specific occasions.

I have deliberately construed the initial asymmetry in such a way that it is the pupil who asks questions like "What does X mean by 'S'?" The reason for this is that we typically use statements like "X means ..." in situations where we can presuppose that X means *something* by "...."; and this presupposition, if Wittgenstein is right, makes sense only if it is taken to imply that X has already acquired a language. It seems to be odd to say of a child whom we try to teach the rules of addition that he does not mean addition by "plus" if he does not make correct additions. We would instead say that he has not yet learned to add, or that he has not yet grasped the rules or the concept of

addition (which, of course, is always *our* concept of addition). This is
an asymmetry quite different from the one I have discussed above: For
if a teacher says to a child "Now you have learned to add" the child
is quite literally accepted into the community of competent adders,
while if I suppose that "X means P by 'S'", the point is not that I
now take X as a competent follower of P-rules; I rather presuppose
that he is a competent follower of *his* rules and form a hypothesis about
what these rules are. To put it more crudely: "X means P by 'S'" is
typically said by somebody who tries to grasp *X's* concepts — and not
to find out whether X has grasped them. This implies, however, that
"X means P by 'S'" involves a tacit reference not only to my (our)
rules of language, but also to the rules *he* is following, i.e., *his* rules
of language — namely in the sense that he must mean *something;* if
not P, what else could it be? This double reference to rules (to his
and ours) could also be brought out by a Sellarsian reformulation of

> X means P by "S"

as

> "S"s (in his language) are "P"s[13]

(where it is understood that "P"s belong to *our* language) — even if
we do not accept any of Sellars' empiricist conclusions.

Now if it is true that by statements like "X means P by 'S'" we
do not only take X into our community but also let him take us, as
it were, into his community, this, I think, also sheds new light on the
degenerate case I have mentioned above, namely the case where my
"meaning-hypothesis" simply becomes the expression of a presupposition I have to make when talking *with* somebody in our (common)
language; viz., "X means *red* by 'red', *love* by 'love', etc." In this
case there is no problem of translation, explanation or interpretation,
because what the "degenerate" meaning-statement expresses is just
the presupposition of an underlying agreement in language. But, of
course, it is an odd expression, for it has no informational content; it
is an odd way of saying that we use words in the same way, i.e., that
we speak a common language. The degenerate meaning-statement
seems to be something like an idling wheel, of which we can only
understand how it got there if we remind ourselves of the function of

---

[13] Wilfrid Sellars, *Science and Metaphysics* (London: Routledge & Kegan Paul,
1968), p. 97.

the non-degenerate meaning-statements: translations, explanations, interpretations. It seems that if we never encountered the problem of *not* understanding each other, or of disagreeing with each other, there would be no place for words like "understanding" and "meaning" in our language. Let me try to show what this implies with regard to the idea of a solitary speaker.

It has already become clear that statements like "X means P by 'S'" can be asserted with good reasons if there is evidence that X in his use of "S" follows a P-rule correctly — i.e., correctly according to my (our) standards of correctness. The implication of this is that our distinction between "right" and "wrong" with respect to rule following is tied to *our* understanding of these rules, so that we judge as wrong what does not correspond to the rules *as we understand them*. I.e., in our judgments about rule following we use our understanding of the rules as a yardstick for distinguishing between right and wrong. We do not use the words "right" and "wrong" primarily from the point of view of an observer, but mainly to approve or correct what somebody says or does, as for instance in teaching. Now it is important to remember that with regard to rule following interpretation and justification come to an end at certain points; at these points we follow the rule *blindly*. Rule-following is a practice, and it is this practice as one that we have learned which provides us with criteria for distinguishing between right and wrong, between what corresponds to the rule and what does not.

It seems that for a solitary speaker such a distinction cannot exist. For *his* understanding of his rules is — as ours is for us — the measure of what is right and wrong. But then — in contrast to us — whenever he follows his rules blindly he must necessarily be right. There is no possible second voice saying "this is wrong" whenever he feels that what he does is right. Since he cannot have the experience of disagreeing with somebody else, the practice of correcting and approving can have no place in his life. But then it seems that he cannot have the distinction between right and wrong with respect to his own rule following, and consequently cannot have the concept of a rule itself. Having the concept of a rule, however, as I have used the expression here, is indissolubly linked up with having a concept of meaning, of understanding, of truth, and of language. If the solitary speaker does not have a concept of rules, he cannot even believe that he is following rules. Accordingly, he could not explain the meaning of his words to himself or to others, teach them to us, etc. He could not relate to himself *as* a speaker and therefore cannot have the concept of other possible speakers who might learn his language. There is no place for a system of personal pronouns in his "language", no place for a concept of communication, argumentation, etc. and therefore finally no place for all those words the role of which can only be explained by reference to the distinction between their first- and third-person use. (Evidently, then, he could not have words for "pain", "belief", "assertion", etc.) But if all this is true one begins to wonder in which sense one could still claim that the solitary speaker means something when he utters sounds or makes inscriptions; that is, in which sense one could still claim that he speaks a language. For what we call a language here seems to be almost unrecognizably different from what we usually call a language.

The preceding argument was not meant as a proof that a solitary speaker is an impossibility; for it is not even clear what such a proof would have to look like. I have avoided the easy way out of arguing that the language of the solitary speaker could not possibly come into being via a series of ostensive definitions which he gives to himself; for although the argument is true, it applies with equal force to a public language. Instead I have assumed, for the sake of argument, that the solitary speaker *has* developed a language in some sense (however it came about), and have then tried to show what most likely must be lacking in this language. My argument could therefore be understood as a heuristic device for showing what we tend to forget about our language when we conceive of a solitary intentional subject of cognition and of speech. Let me now try to indicate how the critique of the idea of a solitary speaker might be "applied" to traditional philosophical conceptions of a "subject" of cognition.

To do this I first want to draw a distinction between what I see as two different levels of Wittgenstein's critique of traditional conceptions of meaning. On the first level he points to the *holistic* character of language: to understand a sentence means to understand a language. On the second level he points to the intersubjective-cum-practical character of language: to speak a language means to be master of a technique and to understand a form of life. It is already on the first level of critique that certain "intentionalist" conceptions of language are ruled out: we cannot explain how words can have meaning by referring to an intentional subject who *means them* in a certain way. Rather, there must be a language for us to be able to mean something by saying something. For this reason alone it would not make sense to assume that a language could come into being via a series of ostensive definitions. Therefore all those conceptions of a solitary speaker which rest on the presupposition of a full-blown intentional subject as a possible "inventor" of language must be rejected already on this level of critique, and together with it all those conceptions of language which try to explain linguistic meaning in terms of meaning-*intentions*. (It seems that such a conception of language has been very widely held — implicitly or explicitly — by many empiricist as well as rationalist philosophers.) However, the thesis of holism gets its real significance only on the *second* level of Wittgenstein's "critique of meaning", where the conceptual framework of language is related to forms of intersubjective communication and practice. Although the idea of a solitary speaker may appear as questionable already on the first level of critique, because it is usually related to an intentionalist conception of meaning, it begins to appear as *radically* questionable only on the second level of critique. Now it seems to me that something analogous could be said about both Kant's notion of a transcendental subject and the early Wittgenstein's notion of a "metaphysical" subject. Both, I think, are to some extent connected with an intentionalist conception of meaning, i.e., with the idea that language is a means to express (and communicate) thoughts which in some sense are (conceptually) prior to their linguistic articulation. In both cases, however, one could object that this is only apparently so since both Kant and the early Wittgenstein — although perhaps for different reasons — could be said to have a "holistic" conception of meaning. So in both cases we would not really be forced to assume that there is a subject of thinking *prior* to the articulation of thought in language. For the sake of argument I would like to take this objection for granted. Even so, I think, both notions of a "subject of thinking" will not only appear as questionable on the second level of Wittgenstein's "critique of meaning", but as questionable for similar reasons as the idea of a solitary speaker and therefore as its close relatives. Why should this be so?

I want to argue this point in an indirect way, viz., by pointing to the peculiar place which the subject of cognition occupies in Kant's world of possible experience and in the *Tractatus* world respectively. Both Kant and the early Wittgenstein could be said to conceive of cognition in terms of a subject in the singular mode, who confronts a world of objects or facts. This world of objects or facts coincides — for Kant as for the early Wittgenstein — with the world as it is described and objectified by modern natural science. In this world a subject in the philosophical sense cannot appear; the subject is not part of but outside this world, either — as for Kant — as its precondition, or — as for the early Wittgenstein — as its limit. The subject is the point from which the world can be seen *as* a world, but it cannot itself be seen or become an object of experience. Now it seems to me that, in some respects, Wittgenstein's position in the *Tractatus* can be understood as a *radicalization* of transcendental philosophy: by means of a semantic transformation it drives transcendental philosophy to a point where it either becomes indistinguishable from empiricism or where it is forced to go beyond itself to explore the conditions of the possibility of the very subject of cognition. The latter is what the later Wittgenstein could be said to be doing; for he explores those forms of "worldly" *intersubjectivity* which must be presupposed if the idea of a subject of cognition or of speech is to make sense. In the *Tractatus,* in contrast, the idea of this subject has become a mere aporia; for although it must be presupposed as the agency of thought and picturing, it is, at the same time, expelled — together with the picturing relation itself — from the world of facts into the realm of the unsayable. Being the limit of the world, it cannot, strictly speaking, even be thought of any longer as this limit. It seems to me that this is the moment of truth about the transcendental subject in general. For it now becomes clear that in the world constituted by or correlated to this subject there is not only no place for a subject, but that, by the same token, this subject is excluded from the realm of meaningful discourse, i.e., form the realm of possible thematization. A subject, however, which cannot thematize itself cannot relate to itself, it cannot say "I". Consequently it must be either non-reflexive — as the solitary speaker — , or its reflexivity must be grounded in a structure of reality which from the point of view of the transcendental or "metaphysical" subject cannot become visible.

One might argue that what I have pointed out is no more than an analogy between problems concerning the idea of a solitary speaker and problems concerning the idea of a transcendental or metaphysical subject of cognition. But even if it were only an analogy (which I do not believe), it would still be a highly significant analogy. For the world of the solitary speaker, if my arguments are right, must be a "reduced" world in very much the same sense as the world of the transcendental subject. In such a world there is no place for a subject of cognition or speech; but this, I would argue, is not a *possible* world as a possible universe of meaning. To conceive of such a world as possible is, I think, ultimately equivalent to having a physicalist conception of the world.

III

Let me now for a moment come back to the little piece of fiction I have used above. In the initial situation of asymmetry the learner — be it Friday or an anthropologist — can only form hypotheses about "what X means by 'S'". Such hypotheses rest on the presupposition that X *does* speak a language; for only if I presuppose that X follows the rules of *a* language can I assume that what he says makes sense, i.e., that there is a sense to be grasped in the sounds which he emits. This presupposition is akin to Davidson's principle of charity, but it is not equivalent to it, as we shall see. At the beginning the presupposition certainly will work in a more or less Davidsonian way. For as we try to "map" the concepts of a foreign language onto our own, the holistic character of our own linguistic competence and thereby the semantic or truth-structure of our own language is tacitly projected onto the foreign language. It is important, however, that we can learn not only that the projection was done in the wrong way, but also that as a projection it was to a greater or lesser extent mistaken. *That* we can learn this is due to the fact that learning a foreign language is not equivalent to developing a full interpretation of it or a translation theory in our language. To *some* extent it is rather always analogous to a child's learning to speak; and insofar as this analogy holds, it is not our ability to *translate* but our ability to *speak* the foreign language which ultimately confirms our presupposition that there is a language to be learned. The more distant the two languages are from each other, the more learning a foreign language involves becoming introduced to, and becoming familiar with, a different form of life. This is a practical learning process the possibility of which does not require that the two languages have a Tarskian truth structure and corresponding truth conditions in common or that they are conceptually isomorphic at some fundamental level. Learning a foreign language is the acquisition of a practical ability to speak (to communicate in) this language in addition to and in conjunction with the acquisition of an — always incomplete — translator's knowledge; therefore the presupposition that what the foreign speakers utter makes sense does not imply complete translatability nor does it imply that most of what the foreign speakers say is true *simpliciter*. As to translation, it follows from what I have said before that we have to some extent conceptually to dissociate *understanding* a foreign language from *translating* it into our native tongue; for translation or interpretation is as much a *way toward* understanding a foreign language as it is a *possibility opened up* only by speaking and understanding two different languages. Although we may begin with translation, translation in a way becomes possible only at the end; what is in between are not just more attempts at translation, but, at the same time, the *practical* initiation into a foreign language game. Therefore translation may be a *problem* even if we understand a foreign language; the presupposition of translatability should be understood in the sense of an unlimited potentiality for the "fusion of horizons" (Gadamer), not in the sense of a matching of truth conditions for the sentences of any two *given* languages. As to truth, it is quite conceivable that much of what the speakers of another language say is not true *simpliciter* under translation, given what counts as true in my native language; it may, for example, be true only in a qualified sense: for what is true according to *their* standards of truth, may, if translated, turn out to imply falsehoods (given *our* understanding of the world, our concepts of nature or of man, etc.). An example would be the Greek equivalent of the sentence "Poseidon is angry", for which a linguistic observer might find as a truth condition that the sea is very rough; but certainly he would not arrive at an adequate translation in this way, for what the above sentence implies is that the roughness of the sea is a sign of Poseidon's anger, and *this* we would hardly be prepared to call true. I think that corresponding examples could be found if we compare, for example, two successive scientific paradigms. Truth and falsehood, as we all know, are intertwined with each other in the most complex ways in what human beings say, believe, assert, etc. A modified "principle of charity", therefore, would only demand that most of what speakers of a foreign language utter or believe must make sense in *some* way; and of course, we might even find out that it makes *more* sense than what we ourselves say or believe. To modify the principle of charity in this way is equivalent to saying that meaning cannot be explained exclusively in terms of truth conditions. This, however, would be disastrous only if we insisted that our understanding of language must be explicable in terms of a semantic *theory*. I cannot see why this should be so.

To sum up my objections against Davidson:[14] I think that the postulate of a Tarskian "truth-structure" common to all natural languages is neither justified nor necessary. It is not *justified,* since even for our own language it seems to be highly questionable whether its logical form — or an essential or basic part of it — can be adequately represented by first order quantificational logic. Moreover, the critique of the first "dogma of empiricism" would make it seem more plausible to assume that the logical form and the conceptual structure of languages are widely interdependent. The postulate is not *necessary* for the possibility of understanding a foreign language, because understanding what somebody says is not equivalent to *interpreting* it. If I understand somebody's utterance "It is snowing" I do not "interpret" it by assigning truth conditions to it, as an English speaker *might* do if he hears a German say "Es schneit". There is a certain analogy here between the "degenerate" meaning statements I have mentioned above and a sentence like "'It is snowing' is true if and only if it is snowing". While "'Es schneit' is true-in-German if and only if it is snowing" might be said to give the truth conditions of the German sentence for an English speaker, " 'It is snowing' is true if and only if it is snowing" does not give truth conditions for the English sentence at all, but is at best part of an explanation of how the word "true" is used in English. But what is more important is that, because of the practical aspect of learning a

---

[14] My reading of Davidson has been based on the assumption that Davidson takes the existence of language *communities* (and of "language") for granted. Meanwhile I have realized that this assumption was wrong in an important respect (see Donald Davidson, 'A Nice Derangement of Epitaphs', in: Ernest LePore (ed.), *Truth and Interpretation. Perspectives on the Philosophy of Donald Davidson* (Oxford: Basil Blackwell, 1986)). However, I believe that the radical consequences which Davidson more recently has drawn from his own theory confirm rather than invalidate my critique of his position.

language, it is not necessary to assume that to understand a sentence of a foreign language "is to find a sentence which has the same place in the structure of our language that the sentence to be interpreted has in the structure of its language."[15] To find such a sentence we may rather have to change our own language. Translatability in principle does not imply isomorphism with respect to truth structure between any two *given* languages. If, however, understanding what somebody says is not always — and not in general — equivalent to having a translation or an interpretation in Davidson's sense, then to talk about "incommensurable" conceptual frameworks may after all be justified in *some* sense: not in the sense that translation is not possible in principle, but in the sense that truths which are expressible in one language may not yet (i.e., without a change of language) be expressible, or may not be expressible *as* truths, in the other language; or that what appears as a truth in one language may, after translation, be deciphered as a mixture of truth and falsehood in the other language. Pluralism of conceptual frameworks has to be readmitted, not in the sense in which it has been rejected by Davidson with good reasons, but in the sense that there are different ways of talking about the world; ways of talking about the world which themselves may turn out to be more or less adequate, which admit to a greater or lesser extent the expression of truth, so that for the sake of truth we sometimes have reasons to revise our ways of talking. This does not imply that there is an extralinguistic standard of truth; what it rather says is that the language we happen to speak does not provide any ultimate standards of truth and rationality either. In short: it is *neither* true that every way of talking (language, theory, self-conception, picture of the world, form of life) is as good as any other, so that most of what people believe must be true in *their* language and uncriticizable from the outside; *nor* is it true that there is a truth-structure common to all languages, so that most of what people sincerely assert in any possible language must be true *simpliciter*. Truth is not relative to conceptual frameworks; this means, however, not that there is a truth-structure common to all languages, but that

---

[15] Frederick Stoutland, 'Realism and Anti-Realism in Davidson's Philosophy of Language', Part II, *Critica*, Vol. XIV, 42 (1982):34. The articles by Davidson to which I have referred are collected in *Inquiries into Truth and Interpretation*, op. cit.

any conceptual framework may have to be revised for the sake of truth.

IV

Speaking with each other in a common language, I have said, we presuppose of each other that each of us has the ability to follow the rules of our language and, by the same token, I presuppose that what *I* mean by "S" is what *we* mean by "S". As a general presupposition this presupposition may always by disappointed "locally", as it were; for I might find out that "S" is not the correct expression for what X *meant* to say, or that X uses an expression in a way different from mine or from the usual one. Speaking a common language we can in such cases ask for and give explanations or interpretations, correct each other, or sometimes, as in the case of good metaphors, we may just grasp immediately the point of what somebody is saying. Now obviously the "interpretative" handling of divergences in the use of language is only one of two major alternatives open to us; the other one is to deny or to reject what the other says as not true, not justified, not right, not truthful, etc. Since, on the one hand, there exists no clear and unambiguous demarcation line between these two alternatives, there can be too much and also too little charity: we tend to be too charitable with our friends and not charitable enough with our foes. Since, on the other hand, the two alternatives cannot be reduced to each other, we must assume that under ordinary circumstances there is a way to find out which alternative is the right one. Very often, in fact, there can be no reasonable doubt; or if there is a doubt, we can remove it by explaining to each other how an utterance was meant. If, however, there is no reasonable doubt that we use words in the same way — and to speak a common language means that there is a vast number of cases where there can be no reasonable doubt — , our linguistic divergence becomes a disagreement about a truth claim. More generally speaking: on the basis of our agreement *in* language disagreements become possible about the truth of assertions or presuppositions, about the sincerity of avowals, about the correctness of moral judgments or about the adequacy of aesthetic evaluations. It is our agreement *in* language, an agreement which includes an agreement about possible ways of arguing for or against..., about possible ways of finding out whether..., about criteria of rationality, etc., which relates such disagreements also to possible ways of resolving them, i.e., to the perspective of a future rational agreement. It should be noted, however, that even in the case of linguistic divergences within a common language we are not always confronted with a simple choice between exercising charity and putting the other speaker wrong. We may rather have reasons to do both at the same time. Making sense of what somebody says does not necessarily mean putting him right; it may rather also be a way of finding out *where* our deeper disagreements are, disagreements which may be about the adequacy of certain ways of using language as much as they are disagreements about the truth of particular beliefs or judgments. If what I have said about the partial incommensurability of conceptual frameworks is true in general, we should expect that there may be incommensurable ways of talking even within the framework of a common language. In such cases "we do not speak the same language" — in one of the possible senses of this phrase; but if we say this we often assume that there is a *right* way of speaking, or that the other is wrong not at this or that point, but in the deeper sense of being wrong already in his language.

But what is the meaning of "right" and "wrong" here? To answer this question would, I think, be an important step toward explaining how rationality is related to the intersubjectivity of language, and therefore also toward explaining what is demanded by Kant's second maxim of common human understanding. Let me, then, come back to Kant's second maxim. I have called it, together with the maxim of autonomy and the maxim of coherence, a maxim of (the right use of) reason; by this I do not only mean that it would be reasonable to follow this maxim, but that following this maxim in some sense is constitutive of what we call being reasonable, as, in other respects, following the maxims of autonomy and of coherence also is. Why should this be so? I think there is a rather straightforward answer to his question. The answer is that "thinking from the standpoint of everyone else" is a way to secure the intersubjective validity of our judgments; and inasmuch as claims to intersubjective validity are — explicitly or implicitly — involved in what we believe, judge, assert or deny, the second maxim is but a reminder of the norm of public truth which we cannot help but accept as long as we speak a language. (Even telling lies presupposes the acceptance of this norm.) But then it would be a specific kind of incoherence to deny the validity of the second maxim. It is as if one would say "It does not really matter whether my beliefs are true", which seems to involve some kind of grammatical absurdity, since my beliefs are what I hold to *be* true. Consequently there are not only good reasons for following the second maxim; we should rather say that the very idea of having good reasons presupposes the validity of this maxim, so that to argue for its negation would be self-contradictory. I think, although I shall not argue here, that something analogous is true for the other two maxims, so that the three maxims together would express a normative conception of reason which, *as* a normative conception, cannot be denied without self-contradiction. The term "contradiction", as I have used it, certainly would need some clarification (which I cannot provide here); perhaps I should rather speak of a "grammatical incoherence", for the incoherence involved seems to be closer to ones like "I believe that p, but p is not true" or "It is raining, but I don't believe it" (as asserted by somebody) than to the standard form of a logical contradiction.

It should be noted that, even if it is true that Kant's three maxims express a normative conception of reason which cannot be denied without self-contradiction, it is not superfluous to *state* them. For although we can hardly *deny* the validity of these maxims, we can easily *violate* them. The denial of evidence, the suppression of arguments, self-deception, "repression" and "rationalization" (in the Freudian sense) are as many ways of avoiding the truth, all of which, however, presuppose the *standard* of (public) truth. It could be said, therefore, that Kant's three maxims express a normative conception of reason, which must even be taken for granted if our methods of avoiding or suppressing truth are to make sense. The three maxims accordingly provide no recipe for being rational, they rather provide an explication of what it *means* to be rational.

But do they provide an *adequate* explication? My concern here is with the second maxim; the question, then, is whether "thinking from the standpoint of everyone else" is really the kind of thing we do and must do if we care for the intersubjective validity of our beliefs and judgments. How *can* we think from the standpoint of everyone else if this standpoint can no longer be defined as the standpoint of *the* (purified) subject of cognition or the standpoint of a noumenal Ego? It is at this point that I finally want to make an attempt to connect the various strands of my argument with each other.

If we try to understand what "thinking from the standpoint of everyone else" could mean, the only plausible answer, I think, is that it means to think and judge in such a way that what we think and judge could be accepted by everyone else; and this, in turn, implies that we do not overlook or suppress or ignore important arguments which could be put forward against our truth claims by others. So far, I believe, Kant could not have any objections. But now the question becomes how we can "operationalize" this demand. Kant's answer: "by putting ourselves in the position of everyone else", somehow seems to beg the question, although I do not want to deny that what we do when we try to anticipate the arguments or objections of others may often be described as "putting ourselves in the position" of somebody else. But of *everybody* else? I think it is at this point that Kant's transcendental solipsism prevented him from seeing the problem. For, first of all, to consider what others might intelligibly say *is* to put ourselves in their position (the latter is normally not a *means* for doing the former); and secondly, therefore to put oneself in the position of everyone else is the same as making sure that one has not overlooked any valid argument or objection. But how, if not *by* putting ourselves in the position of everyone else, can we make *this* sure? The only possible answer, I think, is: by finding out what the *real* others have to say. If our linguistic competence is a collective one (as I have argued before), the only possible test as to whether we have overlooked any possible objections is to look for the real ones: the intersubjective validity of our thoughts and judgments can only be secured in the medium of intersubjective communication and discourse. Only by exposing our beliefs and judgments to the arguments and objections of others can we find out whether they are what we hold them to be, viz., intersubjectively acceptable.

My last sentence could be interpreted in too weak as well as in too strong a sense; and this brings me to the crucial point. The sentence could be read as the trivial thesis that only experience can show whether others agree with me; and it could be read as the strong thesis that intersubjective agreement (however qualified, e.g., as "rational") is a criterion of truth. Both readings, I think, would miss the point. The first one, obviously, does not say anything, while the second one, for less obvious reasons, says too much. Let me, then, try to suggest a reading which avoids these two extremes.

I have argued before that public communication is the natural "medium" in which our ability to speak a (common) language is exercised and confirmed. As Wittgenstein has observed, our agreement in language must include an agreement in judgments to some extent. If disagreement in judgments is possible (makes sense) only on the basis of an agreement in judgments (which, of course, is also Davidson's point), then in every disagreement there must be a tacit reference to a common (although changeable) stock of rules, criteria of evidence or of validity, paradigm cases, etc., which, on the one hand, make the resolution of disagreements — through arguments, or through further experience — conceivable in principle, and which, on the other hand, are nobody's property. Being nobody's property, these rules, etc., embody the "standpoint of everyone else" within a language community; and as far as they do, the restoration of an agreement in judgments is one of the ways in which the intersubjectivity of language itself is confirmed or restored. To put it negatively: once agreement in certain fundamental matters cannot be reached any more, the intersubjectivity of language has begun to disintegrate. But this does not mean that agreement here would be a *criterion* of truth; it should rather be said that it is a confirmation that we still speak a common language.

So far I have only talked about those agreements or about those possibilities of reaching agreement which are so obvious that philosophers before Wittgenstein have hardly found anything interesting in them; e.g., that the sum of those numbers *is* 507; or that the glass *is* broken; or that all these trees *are* cherry trees; or that I *did* leave the chairs in the garden; or that there *is* sunshine on the top of the mountain; or that she *does* speak some English. The point is not that disagreements in such cases can always be resolved, but that there is a natural way to resolve them, once each of us is in an appropriate situation. In such cases there is a "method" of verification or falsification which, even if we cannot employ it in particular situations, makes sure that, if we cannot resolve our disagreements through arguments, we at least know what they are and why we cannot resolve them for the time being. If we take cases like these as paradigmatic with respect to problems of intersubjective validity, we naturally arrive at a procedural notion of rationality such as has been characteristic not only of the empiricist tradition but also of Kant in his theoretical and moral philosophy.

Only if we move toward the other end of the spectrum, namely toward disagreements of a more substantive kind, this procedural notion of rationality begins to appear as questionable. I am thinking of theoretical disagreements in physics, of disagreements about the interpretation of texts, or of moral, political, aesthetic and philosophical disagreements. In all these cases truth claims — if we take this term in its broadest possible sense — are raised, contested and argued about. Consequently even here disagreements, as long as we want to call them disagreements, must tacitly refer to some common stock of rules, criteria of evidence or validity, paradigm cases, etc. And yet there are evidently no decision procedures. The reason for this, at least very often, is that our disagreements here are more "holistic" in nature than those considered previously and therefore in the end must even affect the rules and criteria mentioned above or the ways we apply them. But then only two alternatives seem to be open to us: either we say that rational argument is not really possible in these cases (the fact that we do argue involves some kind of illusion), or we reject the procedural notion of rationality which led us into the impasse. I would argue that the first alternative has been advocated, e.g., by Max Weber for the field of ethics, by the logical positivists for most of ethics, philosophy and the human sciences, by Kuhn for scientific theories (i.e., for inter-paradigmatic debate) in general, and finally by Rorty as a kind of general strategy for thinking about what is interesting in human discourse. From what I have said before it has already become clear that I want to advocate the *second* alternative. Let me try to point out what is involved in this alternative.

The reason why the first alternative is so tempting is that it links a holistic conception of meaning with a procedural notion of rationality in a peculiar way. Languages, theories, value-systems, forms of discourse are seen as closed systems which are, as it were, self-sufficient — embodying their own criteria of validity, standards of solution, paradigms of truth, or criteria of relevance. Moving *within* the system, we can be rational, which usually means: coherent, while at the limits of the system the notion of rationality becomes undefined: for if meaning and truth are possible only within some system, and if there is no meta-system, encompassing, as it were, all the particular systems, then rationality can always be displayed only within one or the other system. Moving from one system to the other therefore becomes a leap in the dark, a decision, a Gestalt-switch, a conversion, or what have you. As against this I would argue that the idea of a closed system of meanings is a myth; and thus far I would follow Davidson who has criticized this myth as the "third dogma of empiricism". However, as I have pointed out before, I do not want to follow Davidson in making translatability (between any two *given* languages) a condition of meaningfulness. To put it crudely: I want to admit some degree of incommensurability while denying the closure of the systems. The net result of this "double strategy" would have to be a broader conception of rationality.

As to partial or temporary incommensurabilities, I have already argued before that we need not deny them; the presupposition of intelligibility does not imply translatability in the strong Davidsonian sense, but only in the weaker "hermeneutic" sense of an unlimited possibility of a "fusion of horizons". After translation, my language, or their language, or both, may not be the same as before. There is already an indication here that the "truth space" common to all languages extends beyond the confines of any particular language: not as a truth structure common to all languages but as the possibility of extending the truth space of any particular language by changing it from within.

To be sure, this possibility of criticizing and changing a language "from within" *is* the debated issue. So let me try to be more specific. Richard Rorty has recently renewed (and generalized) the old Kuhnian argument, that from within certain ways of speaking about the world (Rorty calls them "jargons") only an accumulation of anomalies can be registered, but that there is no rational way out of such a "jargon" — and therefore out of theäproblems to which it has led — , since as long as we argue on the basis of the criteria of validity and relevance embodied in this jargon we always remain entrapped in it.[16] Consequently, Rorty argues, what really matters is not the critique of old theories, vocabularies, "jargons", etc., but the invention of new ones, i.e., "the formation of alternative systems of belief and desire which cause progress to occur without supplying reasons why it should occur."[17] Rational commensuration, on this view, comes always *post*

---

[16] Richard Rorty, 'Beyond Realism and Anti-Realism: Heidegger, Fine, Davidson, and Derrida.' Unpublished manuscript.

[17] Ibid., p. 13.

festum; it is a matter of the historian who, on the basis of the new jargon, can explain what was wrong with the old one. "Bilinguals emerge, so to speak, only when the fighting is over, when the shades of night are falling over the battlefield and intellectual history begins to compare shades of gray. We need time to figure out how to express bad old problems in good new jargon, precisely because (*pace* Platonism and positivism) there is no pre-existent neutral matrix available for purposes of commensuration. Incommensurability is, on this view, real and important, but temporary."[18]

Now I think that Rorty is right when he claims that only on the basis of new theories, ways of speaking or, if you wish, "jargons" can we effectively criticize the old ones, viz., explain what was wrong with them. I have presupposed as much as this throughout my paper. Rorty is wrong, however, if he puts this in terms of an opposition between rational argument (operating *within* in a system) and irrational — or a-rational — invention. As against this I would argue that it is pre-cisely the insistence on this opposition — in a more Kantian language: the insistence on a sharp boundary line between rationality and imagi-nation — which expresses most clearly the third dogma of empiricism.

Let me try to explain why the opposition is artificial. I think it has by now become clear that the distinction between "normal" and "revolutionary" science tends to break down once we try to explain it in terms of a system-bound procedural notion of rationality: for there is too much in normal science itself which, although quite reasonable, does not correspond to this procedural conception of rationality. Let us, on the other hand, take Einstein inventing the theory of relativity. Did he really, as Rorty would have it, "forget" Newtonian physics to create his new jargon? I do not think that this would be a very illuminating description of what happened; it rather seems that all the great physicists of our century were not only "bilingual" all the time after their great inventions, but that they could not have invented new theories if they had forgotten the old ones. Even Wittgenstein, one of Rorty's crown-witnesses, did not simply dismiss or forget the old questions together with the vocabularies in which they were formu-lated, he rather tried to show what was wrong with them: so his new "vocabulary" got its point from the attempt to put the old problems in a new light.

---

[18] Ibid., p. 10.

Now it is evident that not everybody can be Einstein, or Wittgenstein — or Beethoven, or Picasso. So the point cannot be to simply reserve Rorty's opposition by saying that the only truly rational men are the geniuses: being rational is not the same as being inventive. On the other hand, being stupid has something to do with having no imagination; and can a stupid man be said to be rational? Well, in a way he could; but if we call him rational we are using precisely the narrow conception of rationality which excludes every interesting, new, thoughtful or original way of arguing from the sphere of rational argumentation.   But then, if the man is so stupid that he really *is* unreceptive to all arguments which transcend the confines of his narrow little system, I begin to wonder whether we would really want to say that, although he is very stupid, from the point of view of rationality there is nothing wrong with him.

Obviously, what we have to avoid at this point is to get into a fruitless terminological quarrel. So I am prepared to call the stupid person — even if it be Eichmann — a "rational being". I *surrender* the word "rationality" to Rorty and his philosophical allies (to recapture it later on).   For what I am interested in is not rationality in the minimal sense in which Kant also uses the term when he speaks of human beings as "rational beings"; what I am interested in is, rather, a normative conception of reason, as it is expressed in Kant's three maxims of common human understanding; a normative conception of reason, which rational beings tend to fail to live up, viz., by being intolerant, dogmatic, narrow-minded, by deceiving themselves, being unimaginative, unreceptive to arguments, and lacking good judgment. We might use the word "reasonable" to characterize somebody who is not only a rational being but shows some of the *virtues* of reason. I would then claim that being reasonable has to do with being aware of the limits of one's own conceptual system and being prepared to go beyond them, doing justice to the different perspectives of others and trying to bridge the gaps of incommensurability.

It seems to me that something like this is involved in any serious argumentation and deliberation. Arguments, except for simple cases, do not come in single pieces. The more substantive they are, the more their force depends on a context of explication which we have to make up while arguing. Therefore there is some transgression of boundaries, some little piece of innovation in any interesting, new, or illuminating argument. A good argument is often one which makes us see a situation, or a problem, or ourselves in a different way, *establishing* rather than merely *operating from within* a coherent and intersubjectively shared perspective. Argumentation is more like moving back and forth between different, and sometimes incommensurable, perspectives, *making* them commensurable, than operating from within a closed system of meanings, which on the narrow view of rationality must always be taken for granted if argumentation is to be possible.

My thesis, then, is that argumentation — what we usually *call* argumentation — does not only play a role with respect to preserving and restoring the intersubjectivity of language, but also functions as a medium of *transcending* the confines of particular conceptual systems and of *extending* the space of intersubjective communication. Although the power of rational argument is very limited indeed, the limits of its power are not defined by the limits of conceptual systems; for once we are aware of these limits, we are already beyond them. And although we may sometimes not be able to get out of a language game which has gone bankrupt without the help of a genius — or, for that, a revolution, or a catastrophe, or a psychotherapist — , it is always *we*, becoming bilingual, as it were, who must be convinced that a new way of talking about the world, of formulating problems, of dealing with conflicts, or of relating to other people is *better* than the old one. This "rational commensuration" is not a matter for the historians; or if it is, we must become our own historians. For if we could not give any good reasons whatsoever for why we got from "there" to "here" — i.e., if there *were* no reasons but only causes — we could no longer relate to our own past in an intelligible way: we would *have* no past, but rather would live in the eternal presence of everchanging fashions. Besides, often "those who do not remember the past are condemned to repeat it". It is here, if anywhere, that the internal relationship between Kant's three maxims of common human understanding becomes manifest.

V

Let me come back to my thesis, that the intersubjective validity of our thoughts and judgments can only be secured in the medium of public communication and discourse. This thesis has an interesting content, going beyond that of the private language argument, only in as much as we think of argumentation in the broader sense which I have suggested above. For it is only here that the maxim of thinking from the standpoint of everyone else poses a *problem:* it is the problem of finding out what people have to say who do not speak — exactly — our language. If as speakers we always live in a space of truth which transcends what we might call our own conceptual system, then thinking from the standpoint of everyone else does not mean thinking from the standpoint of everybody who thinks like we do, it rather means thinking in such a way that even those who do *not* think like us might be rationally persuaded by our truth claims. This, however, is only conceivable in the medium of public communication and discourse. Speaking and arguing *with* others, trying to understand them and trying to make ourselves understood, is the only way to test our truth claims as against the unforeseeable plurality of different "standpoints". Precisely inasmuch as our truth claims transcend the boundaries of our own language, of our own way of speaking, of our own conceptual system or our own form of life — and they need perhaps not *always* do that — , they can only be confirmed in the medium of public discourse; a public discourse which now appears as that element in which alone thinking from the standpoint of everyone else becomes possible.

What I have said comes close to some of the considerations which Habermas has put forward in support of a consensus theory of truth. Truth, according to this theory, is the content of a rational consensus; and a consensus can be called "rational" if it has been achieved under conditions of an ideal speech situation. As I have already indicated above, however, I do not believe that a consensus theory of truth and the peculiar account of discursive rationality which goes with it can be justified. Truth, as I have argued elsewhere,[19] cannot be defined in terms of a rational consensus, even if truth, in *some* sense, implies the possibility of a rational consensus. For, to put it in a nutshell: although truth is public, the *recognition* of truth is always *my* recognition: i.e., *each of us* must be convinced by arguments if a consensus is to be called rational; but then the consensus cannot be what convinces us of the validity of a truth claim. It may *confirm* our convictions, for when a consensus is achieved, no objections *are*

---

[19] Albrecht Wellmer, *Ethik und Dialog* (Frankfurt: Suhrkamp Verlag, 1986), pp. 69–102.

raised any more. But neither can it guarantee truth, nor does the fact that objections are raised imply that we must be uncertain about our truth claims. Although truth is public, it is not decided on publicly: I *myself* have to decide in each single case whether I ought to take an argument seriously or not, whether an objection is serious or irrelevant, or whether a truth claim has been justified. In short: it is always "I myself" who have to evaluate what the others say — their truth claims, arguments and objections; and as far as these evaluations are fallible, they cannot become infallible by becoming collective. I find it tempting to say that this "I myself" is the kind of "transcendental subject" which we cannot get rid of; only we must be aware that this subject is not an ultimate substance or an ultimate origin of meaning and truth, but is, as it were, only an *"accidens"* — although an essential one — of an intersubjective form of life. Or, to put it in less paradoxical language: although a space of meaning and truth is only opened up by language, which is basically intersubjective, the notion of truth cannot be separated from those of belief and judgment, which always belong to individual speakers. And although only *together* can we make sure that we understand each other, or that we speak a common language, or that — for the time being — our truth claims are intersubjectively acceptable, even jointly — i.e., as an actual community of speakers — we can never make sure that new problems or objections may not come up in the future. Consequently a consensus, to be a criterion of truth, would have to be conceived as an infinite one; an infinite consensus, however, would be the kind of thing which by definition we could never use as a criterion.

The consensus theory of truth, as it has been developed by Apel and Habermas,[20] tries once more to establish *one* ultimate standard of intersubjective validity. The underlying idea is, that this standard of

---

[20] Habermas has meanwhile pointed out to me that I have falsely attributed a strong criterial interpretation of the consensus theory of truth to him. Given some of his more recent formulations of the consensus theory I accept this objection. A fair discussion of Habermas' theses would have to refer to these more recent formulations of the theory. Some of this can be found in my critique of the consensus theory in the book mentioned in the preceding footnote. Since Habermas' modifications of his theory have so far not convinced me that they can *both* solve the problems involved in a strong criterial interpretation of the theory *and* preserve it as an informative theory of truth (in the original sense), I have, for the sake of simplicity, somewhat unfairly referred here only to the strong criterial version of the theory. It should, however, become obvious to the reader in what follows that

validity, in contrast to all particular standards, criteria, or rules, could never be questioned because it would coincide with the very *notion* of truth. The consensus theory can establish such a standard, however, only at the price of making it inapplicable *as* a standard: in the end we are left with the standards, criteria and rules which we happen to have wherever we are, standards, criteria and rules which may themselves turn out to be questionable as time goes on. This, I think, shows that the rational core of the consensus theory is but an explication of the relationship between truth, reason and intersubjectivity, an explication which cannot possibly give us any ultimate *criteria* of truth or rationality. I agree with Rorty that we cannot have any such ultimate criteria or standards; in contrast to Rorty, however, I do not believe that we *need* them to defend an idea of reason and truth which transcends the limits of any particular language game. The expectation — whether feared or welcomed — that without ultimate criteria of rationality and truth the idea of reason loses its ground, is but the expression of a foundationalism which has not been completely overcome. Foundationalism is the search for an Archimedean point, a point which still gives us a firm stand, when the world begins to move or to disintegrate. Foundationalism, however, is closely tied up with a procedural notion of rationality: when the rules of the game are fixed, as, for example, the rules for chess, there is a decision procedure for finding out whether a move *within* the game is legitimate or not. But this decision procedure evidently cannot be used for finding out whether the rules themselves are the "right" ones or not; this question either becomes meaningless or forces us to move on to a meta-game with meta-rules which then allow us to decide this "meta-question", etc., until we finally *either* arrive at some basic rules which are taken as self-supportive or self-evident *or* come to the conclusion that the basic rules can never be justified, but can only be introduced by *fiat*. As long as we think about rationality and language in terms of such a model, the only choice we have is that between foundationalism, on the one hand, and some form of relativism, decisionism or irrationalism, on the other. However, the model is wrong in the first place; for language is not a system of hierarchically ordered rules, such that if

---

my critique of the consensus theory at this point is more like a strategic device for indicating in which sense I do want to relate positively so some of Habermas' basic ideas about truth and rationality.

a quest for justification is carried far enough, we necessarily arrive at some fundamental level of rules or premises, for which we either have to invent some special kind of justification (a *"Letztbegründung"*, in Apel's terms), or which we have to acknowledge as unjustifiable. Although "justification comes to an end", it does not come to an end in *this* way. For although there are always some beliefs, presuppositions or rules, which are more basic than others, so that, when *they* become questionable, major conceptual reorientations may become necessary, we can never — except in local contexts — point to any ultimate presuppositions which would carry the whole edifice of language, so that, when these presuppositions become questionable, argumentation comes to an end. If our doubts are to make sense, much has to be taken for granted; but what has to be taken for granted are not ultimate premises or principles or criteria of rationality — for the simple reason that there *are* none.

As far as a consensus theory of truth still moves within a foundationalist mode of thinking, I think it cannot be defended. It seems to me, however, that the consensus theory of truth, in particular in the form in which it has been worked out by Habermas, could also be understood as a non-criterial, fallibilistic interpretation of the relationship between truth, reason and intersubjectivity. My interpretation of Kant's second maxim has actually been inspired by such a non-foundationalist reading of the consensus theory. And while I have tried to steer a middle course between Rorty's cheerful and sometimes frivolous skepticism, on the one hand, and the foundationalist leanings of Apel and Habermas, on the other, I have, at the same time, tried to indicate how one might try to reinterpret Habermas' notion of communicative rationality in such a way that even Rorty's best insights in the end might be accommodated by it. A fallibilistic account of the relationship between truth, reason and intersubjectivity would allow us to affirm and defend the tradition of Enlightenment without endorsing the two basic dogmas of empiricism and rationalism: a scientist conception of the world and an algorithmic notion of rationality. This, however, is not only Apel's and Habermas' basic concern; it rather seems to me that much of what Rorty has to say could — or perhaps: should — also be redescribed in such terms. The idea of such a "dialectical" overcoming of opposites may sound too Hegelian; however, it seems that Kant himself had something like this in mind when he thought about the applications of his second maxim in matters of philosophy. In a letter to Markus Herz he writes:

> You know that I do not approach reasonable objections with the intention of merely refuting them, but that in thinking them over I always weave them into my judgments, and afford them the opportunity of overturning all my most cherished beliefs. I entertain the hope that by thus viewing my judgments impartially from the standpoint of others some third view that will improve upon my previous insight may be obtainable.[21]

VI

My remarks in the preceding paragraph are no more than promissory notes, particularly since I have not yet even started to explain how, and in which sense, what I have said about rationality could be applied not only to scientific truth claims, but also, for example, to moral, aesthetic, or hermeneutic validity claims. Throughout my paper I have taken it for granted, not only that where we can argue, truth claims of *some* sort are involved, but also that we *can* and *do* argue about, for example, moral, aesthetic, or hermeneutic matters. How these different truth claims are to be distinguished from each other, how we can argue about them and how they are related to each other — these questions I have not been able even to touch in my paper. Of course, one might argue that these questions are just *different* questions; and in one sense I agree. At the same time, however, it seems that a normative conception of reason as I have tried to defend it would get a specific meaning only if it were spelled out with respect to specific truth claims and their relations to each other. The problem will become clearer if we focus on *moral* truth claims: Habermas and Apel have tried to establish a direct link between a normative conception of reason and a universalist principle of morality. There seems to be something wrong with this, however; for the demand — to stick with Kant's second maxim — to think from the standpoint of everybody else, appears to be compelling only if it is already understood what kind of validity claims are at stake. The nature of moral truth claims cannot be explained solely by reference to the demand

---

[21] Quoted in Hannah Arendt, *Lectures on Kant's Political Philosophy*, ed. by R. Beiner (Chicago: The University of Chicago Press, 1982), p. 42.

of their intersubjective validity. Therefore the implicit universalism of the second maxim, on the one hand, and moral universalism, on the other, cannot be simply identified with each other. Habermas and Apel have tried to circumvent this problem by introducing the concept of a "normative" validity claim as a linguistic universal, i.e, as a validity claim which, together with the validity claims of truth and truthfulness is constitutive of every speech act as such. I do not believe, however, that such "formal-pragmatic" distinctions can lead to an adequate distinction between "validity spheres" — e.g. those of science, morality, and art — and of corresponding modes of argumentation. I have argued this point elsewhere[22]; here I merely want to point to the fact that, if a formal-pragmatic grounding of the distinction between different spheres of validity fails, the concept of moral truth — as well as that of aesthetic validity — must appear as more problematic than it does in the theories of Habermas and Apel. This by no means implies that we cannot speak of "truth" (intersubjective validity) in moral (or aesthetic) matters; what I want to say is merely that the meaning of moral (or aesthetic) validity claims has to be explained on a different basis.

This was not obvious to me when, in an article published eight years ago,[23] I criticized von Wright for sticking to a teleological conception of rationality, which would not allow him to see the direct link between rational argumentation and a universalist morality. Although I soon realized that *something* was wrong with my critique, I thought until very recently that what was right in it was more important than what was wrong. Actually this is what I originally wanted to show in my paper. However, reading *The Varieties of Goodness* again I had increasing doubts whether what I wanted to show would be really a critique of von Wright; for I realized that von Wright was right on one essential point, namely in insisting on a clarification of the meaning of the "morally good" as a precondition for explaining the relationship between rationality and morality, i.e. of what it means to

---

[22] With respect to moral truth claims in Albrecht Wellmer, *Ethik und Dialog,* op. cit.; with respect to aesthetic validity claims in 'Truth, Semblance, Reconciliation: Adorno's Aesthetic Redemption of Modernity', *Telos* No. 62, pp. 89–115.

[23] Albrecht Wellmer, 'Georg Henrik von Wright on "Explanation" and "Understanding" ', in *Contemporary German Philosophy,* Vol. 4, ed. by D.E. Christensen et al. (University Park, London: The Pennsylvania State University Press, 1984). (Originally published in German in *Philosophische Rundschau* 26 (1979): 1–2.)

be rational in moral matters. As a consequence I am no longer quite sure about *how* my arguments are related, if at all, to von Wright's. Still, I do believe with Habermas that we do not understand rationality in its various manifestations if we do not understand how moral or aesthetic "truth"-claims are related to truth claims of other sorts: empirical, theoretical, technical, or hermeneutic ones. For if Kant's three maxims of common human understanding give an explication of what it means to be reasonable, they refer to the unity of our life; and this means they implicitly refer to the task of integrating the various dimensions of truth with each other, in which we cannot help but live all the time and all at the same time. Perhaps one could speak of different "styles" of rationality characteristic of different dimensions of truth, different discourses and different forms of praxis. These different styles of rationality, forms of discourse and forms of praxis are always already connected with each other in our life, presupposing each other, allowing for and often demanding transitions from one to the other. A normative conception of reason, as I have tried to defend it in this paper, would then refer to this complex space of truth as a whole, demanding that we learn to move in it in the right way from one point to the other.[24] Accordingly the reflections which I have presented in this paper are very incomplete indeed; however, I hope at least to have indicated with my final remarks how they might be reconnected with an analysis of the different "dimensions" of rationality as distinct but interrelated manifestations of *one* faculty of reason.

---

[24] This problem has been a *leitmotif* in Habermas' theory of communicative rationality. For an alternative strategy see Martin Seel, *Die Kunst der Entzweiung. Zum Begriff der ästhetischen Rationalität* (Frankfurt: Suhrkamp Verlag, 1985), Chap. IV. See also Albrecht Wellmer, *Ethik und Dialog,* op. cit., Chap. 3, XII.

RESPONSE TO ALBRECHT WELLMER

DAVID COCKBURN

There are cases in which, say, my moral views arise from "subjective and personal conditions" in a way such that we want to say that they are not to be taken seriously. Similarly with other views. When I realise that my judgement of another's character is determined largely by jealousy I can, in an important sense, no longer take my judgement seriously. Now a crucial question here is: What conditions are to count as "subjective and personal" — as idiosyncratic? Until we have an account of this we do not have an understanding of what it is to think seriously — to be aiming at truth. For the attempt to overcome the subjective and personal in this sense is part of what it *is* to be trying to get things right.

It will help, I think, to make a distinction here. Sometimes the charge that "You only say that because you are a man/jealous/a Christian" is the charge that this characteristic has led you to overlook something whose force you would acknowledge if you did have it clearly in mind. Wanting to avoid this is part of what it is to think seriously about something. Now at times Wellmer puts this kind of thing at the centre of the picture in his attempt to bring out what he thinks is correct in Kant's maxim that we must think from the standpoint of everyone else. How, he asks, can one be sure that one has not overlooked any valid argument or objection? "The only possible answer I think is: By finding out what the *real* others have to say" (p. 150). Hence the need for a social context for thought and language. Now this invites the objection that finding out what others have to say is not the only, and sometimes not a very effective, way of trying to ensure that I have not overlooked any valid argument. I can look for arguments myself; and everyone else might miss some. Wellmer does, I think, acknowledge this and so insists that we must be careful how we take his suggestion. But I think we can get more easily to the crucial issue by starting off on another foot.

The charge that I am being influenced in my judgement by personal idiosyncracies can have a rather different force. In some cases jealousy may cloud my judgement of another by simply leading me to overlook certain pieces of evidence. But in other cases it seems to be different. In one sense I take note of everything in his behaviour that others appeal to, but I see it all through jealous eyes. It is not that I quietly forget all of his acts of generosity and the warmth of his smile. Rather, where others see generosity and warmth my jealousy leads me to see something more sinister. I take it this is a common phenomenon — especially in relation to our moral views and our thought about others. It is this kind of phenomenon which I would want to put at the centre of the picture.

In so far as I am aiming at truth at all I try to overcome the influence of such "subjective and personal conditions". That is part of what it is to be trying to get things right. Kant concludes that we must abstract "from the limitations which contingently affect our own estimate" [1] — in so far as my judgement is a reflection of the way I just *happen* to respond to the world it is not to be taken seriously. Wellmer links Kant's suggestion with the idea that all those conditions "which pertain to subjects as empirical, that is, embodied, beings" are to count as idiosyncratic (p. 130). Now in so far as one has any sympathy with a central feature of Wittgenstein's later philosophy this is going to have pretty dramatic implications. If I am to regard all of my reactions to my experience which pertain to myself as an empirical, embodied, being — my spontaneous response to another's smile, my refusal to put my hand in the flame, and so on — as exerting "a prejudicial influence" on my judgement no room will be left for any thought at all. So it seems that we have moved very rapidly from a principle which we are all committed to accepting to the Kantian purified subject and the impossibility of there being any such thing as seriously trying to get things right.

The notion of the personal, of the purely idiosyncratic, does, however, shift in a noteworthy way in this argument. The notion of the idiosyncratic is the notion of something that is peculiar to me. The emphasis is on the way *I* happen to respond to the world. In the argument, however, the emphasis shifts to "the way I *happen* to respond". To put it crudely, the focus shifts from the relationship

---

[1] Quoted by Wellmer, p. 130.

between myself and others to the relationship between myself and the world.

The problem was that of finding an acceptable account of what "purely idiosyncratic" can possibly mean in this context. But once the misleading picture is removed very little problem seems to be left. Serious thought requires that I insulate my judgement from the influence of everything that is peculiar to *me* — marks me off from others. We might tentatively suggest that the relevant others are those to whom what I say is, in some sense, addressed. This leaves open big questions to which I will return in a moment.

The idea that the serious seeker after truth must not allow his thought to reflect any of the ways in which he just *happens* to respond to the world holds great charm for philosophers. It is not now difficult to see why. In so far as our ideal is that of the solitary seeker after truth, in so far as we are not operating with *any* conception of an audience for our words, no room is left for our normal notion of what is idiosyncratic in our thought. That leaves us with a choice. We can abandon the notion of the purely subjective and personal and so leave ourselves no room for the notion of trying to get things right. Alternatively, I can regard all of the ways in which I *happen* to respond to the world as idiosyncracies — influences to be eliminated from my thought — and so leave myself with nothing to *get* right. I am inclined to say that the requirement which leads to this is simply a muddle arising from a failure to recognise the framework within which a notion of truth has a place. But I do feel slightly nervous about that suggestion.

I would approach the issue of the solitary speaker with considerations of this kind in mind. My conclusions would, I think, be the same as Wellmer's. I am not sure whether my argument would be of just the same form as I do not completely follow his response to McGinn. It seems to me that in accepting the idea that language is essentially a rule-governed activity he makes things more difficult for himself that they need be. I will not pursue this beyond asking what he means when he says that "we use our understanding of the rules as a yardstick for distinguishing between right and wrong" (p. 139).

The notion of truth, my idea of myself as trying to get things right, is necessarily connected with a conception of what are to count as "personal and subjective" influences on my thought. And this notion, I suggested, needs to be explained in terms of what marks me off from others. I spoke of the relevant others as being those to whom what I say is addressed. This might be better put by saying: those to whom it must be possible to make what I say acceptable. The difference between trying to get things right and merely giving expression to, say, my dislike of beetroot lies in the fact that in the first case I have a conception of others to whom what I say could be made acceptable. Now Wellmer suggests that we must "think and judge in such a way that what we think and judge could be accepted by everyone else" (p. 149). By "everyone else" I think he means "all other possible speakers". In any case, the demand seems to go clearly beyond anything suggested by Wittgenstein — and in a variety of ways. Wellmer agrees with that. It is, however, not clear to me why he thinks it is a necessary requirement. The notion of truth is tied with my having *some* conception of a relevant audience for my words. But why this one?

Wellmer argues that some of the reasons which have been given for thinking that universal rational consensus is impossible are based on faulty pictures — a far too narrow conception of reason, a misleading picture of self-contained language games. While I have great sympathy with much of what he says here we still need positive reasons for thinking that striving for rational consensus is part of what it is to be rational.

The claim that meaning cannot be explained entirely in terms of truth conditions might be expressed by saying that philosophers who think in terms of truth conditions are operating with an extraordinarily narrow conception of the data which are available to the radical translator — as if all we had to go on was the fact that they produce this sentence when, and only when, the sea is rough (cf. p. 144). But, of course, we can, and must, also look at the way in which their words fit into other things that they say and do. And the fact that adequate translation is impossible is the fact that, our life being very different from theirs, there is no place in it for words carrying that meaning. Given this, there is no place at this level for a dialogue about what they say — questions about the truth or falsity of what they say simply cannot arise for me. (In this connection I am unclear what Wellmer means by the phrase "true *simpliciter*".) Of course, I might move to another level — begin to look critically at either our life or theirs. Sometimes, no doubt, this is what I *ought* to do. And I might conclude that one of us is, as Wellmer puts it, wrong "in the deeper sense of being wrong already in his language" (p. 148). But do I slip into some kind of incoherence if, in other cases, I do not take this step?

Rational consensus among all speakers, in the sense I think Wellmer has in mind, does seem to be *possible* if we are prepared to take a certain attitude towards ourselves. If a woman says to me "You only say that because you are a man" I might it seems reply "I wasn't addressing you". But I don't. I regard this, that I am a man, as a subjective and personal influence on my thought — an influence to be eliminated in so far as I am trying to get things right — at least in certain contexts. I could, on the face of it, regard in this way much more than I normally do. Now to judge in ways that could be accepted by all other speakers would be to regard, for example, the fact that I am a member of this culture as a subjective and personal influence on my thought — in so far that is as this culture has features which could conceivably be lacking in another. It would, I suppose, be to regard the fact that, as we say, I am not colour-blind as a subjective and personal influence. The details in all of this are difficult. It is the task of a certain kind of metaphysics to work them out. But the general outlines of the picture of the world with which I will be left are familiar enough. It is not uncommon for philosophers to hold that something like this is the way the world really is. In so far as this is a reflection of a moral insistence that we should try to make the ways in which we all speak commensurate with each other the suggestion need not, perhaps, involve any confusion. One who makes this demand will hold that in so far as my thought is shaped by what we could call "cultural idiosyncracies" it cannot be regarded as a serious attempt to get at the truth. And just as the world disappears altogether if I am to take all of the ways in which I just *happen* to respond as biasing influences, so it shrinks radically if I am to take that which is necessarily common to the lives of all speakers as my picture of what is not a biasing influence. We could say: Just as a being with no life — the purified subject — has no world, so a being with this minimal life has a minimal world.

A conception of truth seems to have interesting connections with moral considerations here. But my point is that it *is* moral considerations which are involved. It isn't the notion of truth that requires us to think from the standpoint of everyone else. Rather, the requirement, if we make it, entails that conception of truth. And there seems to be no necessity in our imposing that requirement on ourselves.

Towards the end of his paper Wellmer suggests that we must get clear about the notion of truth — in the case he discusses, of moral truth — before we ask questions about the kind of agreement which we should expect to be able to reach in moral matters. I do not know what kind of getting clear could be involved here. In any case, someone who thinks he does understand this is, I think, likely to be sympathetic to Kant's maxim in those cases in which the notion of truth does have a place. But equally, I do not see what objection can be left to the idea of the essentially solitary speaker.

I think there is another way in which Wellmer gives the notion of truth a too central place in his thought. He notes that he takes "it for granted not only that where we can argue, truth claims of *some* sort are involved, but also that we *can* and *do* argue about, for example, moral, aesthetic, or hermeneutic matters" (p. 161). We do argue about morality. We think there are good and bad reasons for holding moral views, reasonable and quite indefensible positions and so on. What about the notion of truth? Well, sometimes no doubt we think there is only one possible way to go on an issue and sometimes we don't. Perhaps I am prepared to assert with confidence what should be done. But I recognise that there are other possible views which I wouldn't regard as foolish and I believe that there is nothing more I could say which would bring others round to my way of looking at things. There is room for argument here but (or so we suppose) it may break down before we reach consensus. Are we to speak of truth here — assuming that things are as we take them to be? Are we to say that I hold my view of the matter to be the *true* one? Some philosophers have strong views on this kind of thing. If things really are as I have described them the notion of truth, they feel, is quite out of place. I am inclined to say that there is nothing wrong with this suggestion apart from the insistent tone with which it is made. We can if we choose mark the fact that rational consensus is impossible by saying that the notion of truth has no application. Whether we do or not makes no difference to the facts as I have described them. That we accept, and expect, such breakdowns in some cases but not others does not reflect some more fundamental difference between the cases.[2]

---

[2] While I have concentrated on the case of moral judgements I believe that these considerations are relevant in a wider area. Lars Hertzberg has argued in detail that similar points arise in connection with our ascriptions of psychological states and that this has important implications for our understanding of the place which the notion of agreement in judgements has in Wittgenstein's treatment of language. His most relevant work on this topic is, as yet, unpublished.

NOTES ON THE CONTRIBUTORS

LILLI ALANEN is Research Fellow at the Academy of Finland and Assistant Teacher in Philosophy at the University of Helsinki.

DAVID COCKBURN is Lecturer in Philosophy at Saint David's University College, University of Wales.

ANTHONY KENNY is Master of Balliol College, Oxford.

NORMAN MALCOLM is Susan Linn Sage Emeritus Professor of Philosophy at Cornell University, and Visiting Professor of Philosophy at King's College, University of London.

JAKOB MELØE is Professor of Philosophy at the University of Tromsø.

THOMAS NAGEL is Professor of Philosophy at New York University.

FREDERICK STOUTLAND is Professor of Philosophy at St Olaf College.

ALBRECHT WELLMER is Professor of Philosophy at the University of Constance.

PETER WINCH is Professor of Philosophy at the University of Illinois at Urbana/Champaign. He was formerly Professor of Philosophy at King's College, University of London.

G. H. VON WRIGHT is Research Professor Emeritus at the Academy of Finland. He was formerly Professor of Philosophy at the University of Cambridge and at the University of Helsinki.

INDEX OF NAMES

SUBJECT INDEX